# Climbers and Wall Plants

# Climbers and Wall Plants

including Clematis, Roses and Wisteria

*Peter Q. Rose, NDH*

BLANDFORD

Blandford

an imprint of
Cassell
Artillery House, Artillery Row
London SW1P 1RT

First published 1982
First paperback edition 1990

**British Library Cataloguing in Publication Data**

Rose, Peter Q.
    Climbers and wall plants.
    1. Gardens. Climbing plants
    I. Title
    635.9'74

    ISBN 0-7137-2158-8

Photographs by Robin Fletcher

Distributed in the United States by
Sterling Publishing Co., Inc.,
387 Park Avenue South, New York, NY 10016-
8810

Distributed in Australia by
Capricorn Link (Australia) Pty Ltd
PO Box 665, Lane Cove, NSW 2066

Printed in Great Britain by
The Bath Press, Avon

# Contents

# Foreword

Anyone who has travelled into the forests of Asia and North America will have noticed the strong presence of climbers there. They are an important element in the forest vegetation and, from an ornamental viewpoint, can be quite spectacular. Such plants, however, are not necessarily restricted to a life in the trees, and there are hosts of others which carpet the ground or clamber into and over the scrubby vegetation common to steep hills, ravines and woodland clearings.

Such situations can be very rich indeed, and from my own experience I particularly recall a roadside bank in Western China where six different climbers competed for attention, garlanding the surrounding scrub with as colourful a display as one could wish for. Considering the wealth of plants which grow naturally up supports or which may be conveniently trained to do so, it is puzzling if not depressing that the gardening public does not make full use of such plants. If the answer is merely unfamiliarity with the subject then this book will go a long way towards resolving the situation. If the gardener pleads ignorance then likewise it will help clear the air. For, although Peter Rose's account is by no means the last word, it is by far the most satisfying treatment I have seen for many a year.

It is eminently a practical account which will help those who are considering planting climbers. Here is all the information one will need to help choose the right plant for the right place and, once correctly planted, to care for its future. Such is the author's fascination for his subject, however, that he has garnished the essential practical details with stories and reminiscences concerning the origins etc of the plants so well described.

When I look through my window at the outside world I see bare walls, fencing and sundry supports which would gain from the embrace of a climber. With Peter Rose's help, perhaps the drab accoutrements of man's urban sprawl will take on a new and pleasant aspect.

Roy Lancaster

# Preface

A number of books have been written on climbers and wall plants, but this one differs in giving more details as to the origins of the plants and stories of their introduction. I have done this in the hope that it will for the reader, as it does for me, make the plants live, seeing them as products of history as well as nature, and wondering as to the personalities of the plant collectors, explorers, missionaries, colonial administrators and others who sent plants back to Britain, carefully nurtured perhaps in ships' cabins or carelessly overlooked by hard-pressed sailors on long and often dangerous voyages. Their descendants, the plant collectors of today, no less eager and certainly no less knowledgeable, have the advantage of jet travel; but, unhappily, they are more restricted as to the countries they can enter freely than were their Victorian counterparts, who operated when British citizenship opened the door to any country in the world.

The book's initial chapters comprise the uses and cultural needs of climbers and wall plants, and the alphabetical descriptions which follow show the wide variety available. Although some species may not be easily obtained at the average garden centre or store they are quite likely to be found at specialist nurseries. I do not propose to suggest sources of supply, since these can easily fluctuate by reason of change of ownership or policy. Enquiry can always be made of the Royal Horticultural Society, who themselves run a garden centre that often bristles with less common genera and varieties. Indeed the advantages of the comparatively cheap membership of the Society are so many that no serious, or even partly serious, gardener can afford not to be a member.

In several instances I have pointed out the folly of buying cheap plants. Always buy from reputable nurserymen who will either have grown the plants themselves or who will know and have complete faith in those from whom they have purchased. This is not to say that plants are expensive — far from it. For example a *Chimonanthus* at £8 will give pleasure winter after winter for up to 40 years, an annual cost of 20 pence. A wisteria costing, as it should at the time of writing, around £15, will give its glorious sheets of bloom for 37½ pence a year over the same period.

Books nowadays often have a readership extending outside their country of origin and this is one reason for giving in many cases an indication of the plant's hardiness according to the American zoning system; a zone map and temperature chart are also included. Apart from American interests, this zoning is a guide to all who garden in continental climates and indeed is a useful indicator in Britain, but with any such recommendations the possibility of local factors creating 'micro-climates', favourable or unfavourable, must be borne in mind. Quite small features, hills, slopes etc, can create favourable situations often noted and utilised by earlier builders of dwellings who were more dependent upon natural shelter than we are today. Urban areas, often needing climbing plants to furnish bare walls, sometimes provide a suprisingly congenial climate. Some species will grow in London but not survive some miles further south where in theory the temperature should be higher. The effect of the benign Gulf Stream upon northern Britain's west coast is well known and some of the more tender plants listed in this book do extremely well in those areas.

Finally I have made no attempt to compromise on the use of Latin names and for good measure have included the family names for the benefit of those interested. Common names have been incorporated where they seem to be of value, but I resolutely refuse to call *Forsythia* 'Golden Bells', preferring to recall in the plant's Latin name that grand gardener William Forsythe. The binomial system of plant naming, the creation of Carl Linné (1707–78), or 'Linnaeus', as he Latinised his name, gave to botany, gardening and the biological sciences a unique system of identification and reference that is truly international. Quote the Latin plant name *Laburnum* to a nurseryman in Holland or Honolulu and you will get that plant; ask for 'Golden Chains' and heaven knows what you will receive.

Finally reference is made in many of the descriptions to various plant collectors. These were men, often Kew-trained gardeners, with the scientific and botanical knowledge which that training implies, who were selected and employed to collect on behalf of wealthy horticultural patrons, institutions such as Kew and the Royal Horticultural Society or the great nurseries of the day such as Veitch's. The stories of their lives and adventures have been detailed elsewhere but in considering the plants we grow to embellish the walls of our houses and the borders of our gardens it is fitting to recall the debt we owe them and the dangers they faced so that Britain and British gardens might hold the wealth of temperate climate plants that we grow today.

'No man is an island' is a saying which applies particularly in the writing of a book such as this, and I acknowledge very readily the facts and knowledge gleaned from many sources, in particular the books listed in the Bibliography. In addition, those invaluable publications, *Curtis's Botanical Magazine*, the *RHS Dictionary of Gardening*, the journals of the RHS and *The Plantsman* have been consulted extensively. Suggestions and help from my wife and the interest and expertise of the editorial staff of Blandford Press have made the writing of this book a pleasure which I hope the reader may now share.

Peter Q. Rose

# Introduction

The history of cultivated and ornamental plants is extensive and detailed, yet little is recorded of climbing plants on houses or house walls until the eighteenth century. Old prints and records frequently show climbing plants on fences and arbours and fruit trees on walls but not on houses. One can readily understand that while houses were fortified, and while there might be any threat of attempts to scale the walls to make an entry, no climbing plant which might provide hand or foot hold would be tolerated. With more peaceful times it can be assumed that house walls came to be used for sheltering fruit trees, and that later their capacity for protecting ornamental plants was utilised. Certainly by early Victorian times prints of mansions and cottages show extensive use of climbing plants, and the planting of *Magnolia grandiflora* against rectory and vicarage house walls was so frequent as to lead one to suppose that it sprang from some ecclesiastical directive!

What is meant by 'climbers and wall plants'? A climbing plant is one whose stem at maturity cannot support its plant growth vertically, so that it must either scramble along the ground or lift itself by climbing. The means of climbing are various. Some plants, honeysuckle or wisteria for example, have stems that twine around any solid support of suitable dimensions. In this connection it is interesting to note that plants with twining stems do not all twine in the same way; some such as honeysuckle and the hop plant twine clockwise, others, *Convolvulus* for example, anti-clockwise. A lot of botanical thought has been devoted to trying to find out why this should be so, but at present no solution has been found. Geographical situation has nothing to do with it; a climber that twines clockwise in the northern hemisphere twines in the same manner when grown in the southern hemisphere.

Other climbers such as clematis and nasturtium have leaf stalks that have the ability to grip and twine onto twigs, wire or any small support. In the case of sweet peas and vetches, one or more of the leaflets are metamorphosed into tendrils which grip on to any twiggy support. It is interesting to watch the young tendrils over a day or so whilst they extend rapidly in growth and move in the wind until the sensitive tip comes into contact with a support. Some plants have a refinement of this technique, and after making contact actually build a 'spring' into the tendril by making spirals in the lower part. Should wind tug at the plant, the tendril acts as a sophisticated 'plant tie' able to give with the strains put upon it. Some plants, such as climbing roses, have backpointing thorns enabling them to edge their way up through bushes. Yet others have small adhesive pads (Virginia creeper is an example) that clamp onto trees or rocks in nature and in a garden situation to walls which they can then cover with a close mat of leaves. Others, such as ivy, produce small rootlets capable of embedding themselves in the interstices of tree bark or of walls, and thereby cling tightly to their host, albeit without drawing nourishment from it. There are others, the true vines (*Vitis* spp), for example, that bear lateral shoots which twist spirally 'around foreign bodies', as one of the older botanical textbooks charmingly phrases it. From this brief description it will be seen that the climbing devices of plants are many and various.

These then are the 'climbers'; what of the 'wall plants'? This is a totally artificial term that means what it says, plants suitable for growing on or against walls. It is a wide definition which can encompass several types of plant. Firstly, there are those that in temperate climes need the shelter of a wall in order to flower, for example the Passion Flower (*Passiflora*) or maybe plants such as the Pineapple Broom (*Cytisus battandieri*), thin-rooted and rather easily blown over in exposed situations but firm and flowering more regularly when tied on a south or west wall. Secondly, there are plants which will grow perfectly well in the open, Wintersweet (*Chimonanthus*) for example, but whose early-flowering presence on house walls gives the occupier a foretaste of spring, a foretaste that can be savoured without going out of doors! Finally, others such as *Forsythia*, *Pyracantha* and variegated ivy are colourful or good to look at and useful to clothe a wall, although it is not at all necessary for their growth.

From the foregoing it will be seen that the plants of this book's title can give an added dimension to any garden, large or small.

They comprise some of the loveliest plants available to gardeners, and it is interesting to recall that artistic representations of house exteriors in plays, films, novels or paintings almost invariably depict some form of plant covering on the walls. The balcony beneath which Romeo pours out his heart to Juliet is invariably embowered with greenery of some kind. Cottages in novels have roses and clematis; stately homes their magnolias. In short, art recognises the virtue of walls clad and beautified with plants. In practical terms it has been realised for many years that the imaginative use of climbing plants on walls and trees provides colour and interest, often at times of year when flowers in the garden are scarce. In the chapters that follow I have endeavoured as well as describing the various kinds to include as much information as possible on their history, introduction to Great Britain, characteristics and so on. Any walk around a garden is made more pleasant for visitors if the host can impart this kind of detail; such information can often interest even those whose liking for plants is minimal as well as enhancing the enjoyment of the true garden lover or plantsman.

# Uses in the Garden

Climbing plants in whatever way they are used give an added floral dimension to any garden; beauty of flower or leaf can be presented in varied situations and at various levels, in some cases to attract the eye, in others to efface some unsightly object. The situations where climbers and wall plants can be used to good effect may be summarised as follows:

1) walls and house walls;
2) pergolas and arbours;
3) tree-supported climbers;
4) screening of buildings or sheds;
5) boundary fence cladding.

In this chapter some of the ways in which the plants can be used are described; detailed lists are given on pp. 153–6 whilst the characteristics of the plants mentioned are included in the plant descriptions in the main part of the book.

## Walls and House Walls

A number of shrubs that are very suitable for growing against walls are not climbers; whereas some of them appreciate wall protection others will grow perfectly well in the open shrubbery. *Pyracantha* is frequently used as a wall plant, particularly for north and east walls; it stands clipping, is pleasant in flower and lovely in berry. The Wintersweet, *Chimonanthus praecox*, will grow perfectly well in the open, but its sweetly-scented flowers can perhaps be better appreciated if it is on a house wall, particularly on a cold miserable January afternoon! The pink Acacia-flowered *Robinia hispida*, a whole range of lovely blue *Ceanothus*, the curious Fuchsia-flowered Gooseberry, *Ribes speciosum*, the Pineapple-scented Broom, *Cytisus battandieri*, slightly tender buddleias such as *B. crispa*, and even camellias, all can make first-rate wall plants.

14

USES IN THE GARDEN

Many climbing plants produce flowers at and about their top-most shoots. From nature's point of view this is perfectly logical. Plants with the flamboyant flowers that we like and cultivate, such as clematis, are in fact trying to attract bees and other insects for the fertilisation of their flowers. For this purpose the flowers must be on display, in the sunlight and the air. This tendency to flower on shoots at a high level often leaves lower areas of bare dull stems. At first sight this would seem to be a grave disadvantage to the gardener but it can be turned to advantage; thoughtful placing of wall plants at the foot of those climbers that thrust towards the sun gives the best of both worlds. Often the wall plant can be of a contrasting colour. For example one can plant purple or blue Jackmanii-type clematis with the grey-leaved, yellow-flowered *Senecio* 'Sunshine' set in front. The *Senecio* will make a pleasant rounded bush of about 3 ft (1 m) high hiding the bare lower stems of the clematis. In order that the roots do not compete for moisture and nourishment the clematis should be planted to one side and about 2 ft (60 cm) from the *Senecio*, and care should be taken to train it towards and up through the *Senecio* which should be planted near to the wall. In contrasting manner the wall can be clad with the yellow-green leaves of the ivy *Hedera helix* 'Buttercup', and shoots of a clematis such as 'Perle d'Azure' encouraged to clamber up to display its light blue flowers against the lovely background. Once again the clematis should be planted to one side and some 2 ft (60 cm) away from the ivy so that the roots do not compete. Another ivy, *Hedera helix* 'Sulphurea', with soft grey-sulphur coloured leaves, makes a superb foil for the crushed-strawberry colour flowers of *Clematis* 'Hagley Hybrid', planted in similar manner. The ivies retain leaves down to the base and serve to conceal the bare lower stems of the clematis.

An excellent shrub for north or east walls is *Cotoneaster horizontalis*. Curiously flat, fish-bone style, wall-hugging branches are covered with small pink flowers in May followed in September–October by red berries. For a contrast plant against the wall, some 2 ft to one side of the *Cotoneaster, Hedera helix* 'Glacier'; this has leaves of silvery grey and will climb up through the *Cotoneaster* to make a lovely foil for the red berries.

In choosing climbing or wall plants it is necessary to bear the wall colour in mind. That fine dark red climbing rose 'Guinee'

15

planted against a red brick wall can be 'colour lost', becoming just another red rose easily overlooked by the observer. Against a whitewashed wall it is superb, the flowers standing out and the dark red colour seeming almost black. Blessed are they who garden among grey or honey-coloured stone walls, the Cotswold background that deals as gently with flowers as it does with its occupants. It is a lovely backing for all colours, except perhaps whites and creams. Fortunately nature is kind to gardeners and many white-flowered wall-suited plants such as *Osmanthus delavayii* or *Choisya ternata* supply their own background of ample green leafage against which the white flowers show up so well irrespective of background.

Very few houses nowadays are built with the delightful white painted weatherboard still seen on some cottage homes, particularly in Kent. Although wood is an easy subject to which to attach and nail climbers structurally and aesthetically this is unwise; far better to make use of this lovely background by planting wall shrubs, especially those of somewhat rounded contours such as the lovely blue *Caryopteris*, the pink-flowered purple-leaved *Weigela* or the curious and attractive yellow-flowered *Phlomis fruticosa*.

## Pergolas

The word 'pergola' is derived from the Italian *pergula* meaning 'over-shadowed like an eave'. This Italian origin should warn us that a pergola proper is indeed more suited to sunny climates where covered ways and arbours give grateful shelter from a hot sun. Too often in Britain a pergola can become a dank tunnel of vegetation in which the gardening voyager is dripped upon after every passing shower.

A well made pergola can be a delightful feature, but the first lesson to be drawn from the above observations is not to create the pergola over a main path or route; let it be a secondary path or way that can be ignored or bypassed in inclement weather. Secondly do not plant it with over-vigorous subjects; if they grow well they will thrust upwards and flower primarily on the top, creating only a darkened thoroughfare for the gardener or visitor.

The best and most lasting pergolas are made of stout brick pillars 1 ft or 18 in (30 or 45 cm) square, linked at the tops with stout wood cross pieces laterally and longitudinally (*see* Fig. 1). A cheaper, and very good, version may be made using railway sleepers as uprights (it will be a sad day for British gardeners when all the timber sleepers are gone!) and stout 2 × 8 in (5 × 20 cm) cross pieces. The climbers chosen should be fairly thin growing subjects; climbing roses and clematis are obvious choices. If you are prepared to undertake systematic pruning and training, wisteria and laburnum, flowering as they do virtually together, can make a wonderful picture of yellow and purple. The wisteria planted against one of the supports will twine without difficulty but will need pruning to keep it within bounds and promote flowering. Laburnum is not a climber but can be trained to lovely effect. Plant a standard 6 ft (1.8 m) laburnum against one of the supports, tying the stem to the support at intervals. Ties must be firm but of a kind that permits the stem to grow in girth. The top shoots as they develop should be trained and tied to the undersides of the cross pieces. After a year or so a virtual roof of interlacing branches will be formed bearing

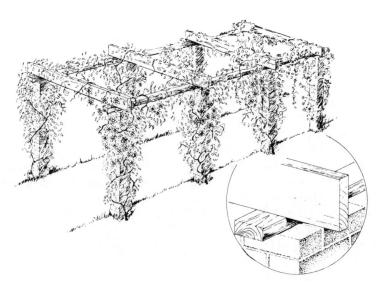

*Fig. 1  A pergola, with the method of construction shown in detail.*

17

masses of golden flowers. The best cultivar for the purpose is *Laburnum vossii* whose flower trusses can be 10 in (25 cm) long.

An extension of this idea is the laburnum walk. Such a walk festooned with golden yellow flowers can be a wonderful sight. Large gardens can accommodate an arched walk of 100 ft (30 m) or so but a lesser scheme can be equally attractive in a small garden and fairly easily achieved. The arch needs to be carefully sited; it should not span a main walk or path since as pointed out earlier overhead structures and plant growth will continue to drip after any passing shower. It can, however, make a most effective link from perhaps the more formal part of a garden to a less formal or different section. There is a fine example of such an arch at Hampton Court Palace Gardens but structural changes over the years to cope with modern demands now have it leading triumphantly to the ladies' lavatory! Luckily, you have more control over the siting in your own garden. In creating this feature several points must be borne in mind. The best support is a curved arching iron frame, expensive these days and few gardeners could contrive such a structure on a do-it-yourself basis; however, a plain timber structure on the lines of the pergola suggested above is within the capacity of most and will serve well. The type of laburnum planted will depend on the style of arched walk required. If it is intended as a 'tunnel', i.e. with the sides filled in with growth, you should procure 'bush' laburnums (plants that have been budded or grafted at ground level and allowed to throw out 3 or 4 side shoots) or alternatively 'Feathered Maidens', i.e. plants with stems 4 to 6 ft (1.2–1.8 m) with buds or developing shoots on the whole length of stem. These are planted 4 ft (1.2 m) apart each side of the archway and trained upwards and sideways so as to cover the arch with growth. If, however, the archway is of a type where the 'walls' are to be open, either for access or for visual effect, then plant standard laburnums, that is those with a completely bare stem and just a head of growth at the supporting pillars or iron work at 6 to 8 ft (1.8–2.4 m) intervals. Whatever the type planted, the shoots as they develop must be trained always under the top bars or cross pieces; they will always try to ascend and if trained above will have to be tied down, and such ties, however strong, will always be a problem. No pruning is needed but shoots should be trained when young and tied so as to fill the roof evenly.

Something which is almost a variation on a pergola is the rope walk or catenary. For this a series of posts are firmly set in line at perhaps the rear of a border, alongside a path or as a 'see through' boundary. Thick rope, 1 in (2.5 cm) minimum diameter (or chain), is attached to the post tops in draped fashion. The best, indeed one might say the only really suitable, climbers for this purpose are climbing roses. In this situation they are easily pruned and make glorious living garlands of bloom. Plant at the posts and train up with long extension shoots trained along the ropes. The posts can be of trimmed wood or larch posts with about 1 ft (30 cm) of the side branches left, or according to the situation they may be more formal brick pillars.

## Arbours and Summer Houses

These are often pictured as Arcadian structures, ideal places to take tea on those lazy sunlit afternoons that seldom materialise these days but seemed to abound in the Edwardian era. Pursuing this image it follows that plants used for coverage should be summery, fragrant if possible and sufficiently twining and luxuriant to give shade from the summer sun and even shelter from the passing shower. This is no place for rigid and thorny *Pyracanthas* but rather for fragrant honeysuckles. Our own native *Lonicera periclymenum* is not to be despised; the clone 'Serotina' (also known as 'Late Dutch') flowers profusely in July. Others worth considering are *L. x americana*, fragrant and white from the end of June and into July, and *L. japonica* 'Halliana', virtually evergreen and flowering continously from June to the autumn.

A summer spot such as this is the ideal site for climbing roses of character, for some of the treasures grown and described in paint and prose by the arch priest of the lovely Old Roses, Graham Thomas. These are fragrant summer-blooming roses such as *Rosa longicuspis* with masses of white banana-scented flowers; 'Wedding Day', richly-scented, yellow in bud opening creamy white; 'Francis E. Lester', white, scented and lovely; 'Françoise Juranville', pink and frilly; or 'Climbing Cecile Brunner', with its masses of shell pink exquisitely miniature roses. Looking back to that soft Edwardian era the summer-

19

flowering *Jasminum officinale*, white and fragrant, must have been a traditional president at those sunlit afternoon teas. Like all the above-mentioned plants, it will provide ample coverage and will not need pruning other than cutting back if it becomes intrusive.

## Screening of Buildings or Sheds

If all sheds, garages and outbuildings were gems of architecture there would be little call for climbing plants; happily for the nurseryman this is not so. Many people must at some time have had the need and urge to plant a climber to cover some wretched but useful shed or ghastly garage. Fortunately there is a fair selection of climbing plants equipped to conceal any lack of architectural skill (or perhaps its total absence), or to cover those utility items whose designs would challenge even Leonardo da Vinci.

For these structures luxuriant and rapid growth are vital, and what better than *Polygonum baldschuanicum*, the Russian Vine? It is rampant of leaf and with a bonus of foaming white flowers in September. Once established the plant grows rapidly and in summer the long shoots flare out seeking a support to entwine. *Polygonum baldschuanicum* is, however, deciduous, and unsightly buildings do not go away in winter. For evergreen coverage nothing can equal ivy, and few plants are brighter in winter than the variegated Persian Ivy, *Hedera colchica* 'Dentata Variegata'; this and other variegated ivies make excellent coverage for sheds, apart from being attractive plants in their own right.

For sheer coverage, but unfortunately deciduous, the Virginia creepers are in a class of their own. The term Virginia creeper is rather a loose one; there are a number of species which differ slightly in their modes of climbing. For walls the best species is *Parthenocissus tricuspidata* which climbs by means of tendrils equipped with adhesive pads. Climbing plants are seldom used on public buildings, probably because architects envisage maintenance problems. This is a pity, as many stark factory buildings could have their lines softened and a more favourable environment produced by some partial clothing with climbers. Possibly stark functionalism is equated with efficiency but I doubt the truth of this. A notable exception in the case of public buildings is the massive 'War Room' adjacent to the Admiralty in London. This prominent reminder of the dark days of World War 2 is covered with a close mat of Virginia creeper which in summer completely softens the severity of the building; it is of course deciduous, but the mat of fine stems helps to blur the harshness of the building even in winter.

## Boundary Fence Cladding

As building land gets ever scarcer and more expensive, so developers cut down the areas of garden. Proximity to neighbours and lack of privacy are then inevitable and a fence or screen becomes a necessity. A close boarded fence ensures privacy but can look rather stark; even worse is chain-link fencing. With careful thought either can be turned into features of interest by the use of climbers. Before planting it should be remembered that once covered with verdure it will be impossible to paint or treat a wood fence, so this should be done initially, and if there is a choice not with creosote but with one of the copper-based preservatives. The additional weight of climbers must be considered and it is advisable for a fence to be of concrete posts firmly fixed and then interspaced with wooden panels or boarding.

A close boarded fence will act host to much the same range of climbers as a brick wall, except that some, ivies for example, are less inclined to cling to boarded fencing than to brick. Wall plants can equally be planted against fences but there must be sufficient height to provide a protective backing. The height of the fence will also dictate the choice of climbers. Strong growing subjects should be avoided since overmuch growth may encroach on a neighbouring plot or by its weight pull down the fence. Attempting to check such growth by pruning is to engage in an annual battle and end with a maltreated plant.

Wattle hurdles, hazel or willow, make a pleasant background and have the merit of interstices that facilitate tying and training. They are best stood on a low wall inset at 6 ft (1.8 m) intervals with strong posts of wood or iron to which the hurdles can be fixed with wire.

Chain-link fencing is occasionally used as a garden divider on newly-developed estates. Understandably it arouses aesthetic

21

objections, having strong associations with compounds and penitentiary establishments. Very often the occupier's first reaction is to plant a hedge against the offending object but this has the effect of further reducing the area of what may be a small plot anyway. There is another solution and in fact chain link can be converted into an attractive adornment by thoughtful planting. For this purpose ivies are first rate, they are evergreen, they grow quickly and are amenable to cutting back. With initial training they will spread horizontally along the fence, and unlike a hedge will not impoverish the whole length of fence ground. They should be planted at the post positions where the ground may be too shallow for some plants. When the intervening fence space is ivy-covered, climbers such as jasmine, climbing roses, clematis and climbing annuals may be planted in the widths between the posts. Trained over the ivy background they will show to advantage although by themselves they would not provide the screen that ivy does. In addition to the common English Ivy, *Hedera helix*, attractive in its own right, there are clones such as 'Goldheart' (green leaves with a colourful golden centre), 'Buttercup' (leaves of lime-green yellow), 'Ivalace' (lacy green crimped glossy leaves) and 'Sulphurea' (greyish sulphur-coloured leaves). Clones of the Persian Ivy such as *Hedera colchica* 'Dentata' which has large pea-green leaves, or 'Sulphur Heart', with green leaves generously splashed with yellow, are superb and make a fine showy barrier, but cannot be recommended for fences or walls under 5 ft (1.5 m) in height.

## Tree-supported Climbers

Anyone who has seen *Wisteria sinensis* hanging in curtains of bloom on trees 60 to 80 ft (18–24 m) high at Pyrford Court in Surrey, or *Rosa filipes* 'Kiftsgate' like a superb fountain of flower at Kiftsgate in Oxfordshire, may be inclined to associate climbers on trees with large gardens. This is not so — lovely effects can be achieved in any garden even if only small trees are available. Selection and thought are advisable. Specimen trees should not be used, but dead or unthrifty ones should not be cut down without giving thought to their possibilities as support for climbers; they can be clothed with beauty and the expense and effort of making artificial supports is avoided.

If considering using a dead or dying tree, try to ascertain the cause of its decline. If it is a pear, hawthorn or *Sorbus*, dieback can be caused by Fireblight disease (*see* p. 36). A more insidious disease, Honey Fungus, can kill a wide range of trees and shrubs. If uncertain as to the cause of the decline, it is worth getting an expert opinion. For both the above diseases the only effective cure is grubbing out and complete destruction by burning.

Assuming that the above troubles are not present, aged apple or pear trees make excellent vehicles for climbers. Some climbers such as roses and clematis can live very happily with their tree hosts, as their growth is sufficiently thin to enable the tree still to flower and leaf; others, such as *Lonicera japonica*, *Actinidia*, *Celastrus* and *Vitis* species such as *V. coignetiae*, are sufficiently vigorous as to smother the tree eventually. Many climbers can be tried and a full list is given on pp. 155–6. Indeed the rose 'Dorothy Perkins', notorious for suffering from mildew when trained to a wall, keeps virtually free of this trouble when allowed to scramble up a small tree, projecting its soft pink flowers through the protective branches.

Sometimes by mishap a large tree dies and has to be felled. This can leave a substantial butt of some 18 in to 2 ft (45–60 cm) in height, unattractive and expensive to grub or move. A better solution is to fell the tree down to some 8 to 10 ft (2.4–3 m) from ground level. If one or more plants of the large-leaved variegated colchica ivy mentioned earlier, *Hedera colchica* 'Dentata Variegata' or 'Sulphur Heart', are planted at the base, this will in a few years provide a lovely pillar of green and yellow leafage and as a bonus a veritable bird sanctuary.

# Soil Preparation

In the past the sites of houses, indeed of settlements and villages were dictated by man's needs, a supply of water, protection from the elements and most importantly the quality of the soil upon which the existence of his animals and himself depended. Nowadays we are no longer circumscribed in this way and houses are often built upon land that is horticulturally and agriculturally third-rate.

Although we manage to choose the type of house we live in, it is not so easy at the same time to choose the soil; and the lover of lime-hating rhododendrons may be obliged by circumstance to garden upon the chalk hills of Surrey. This is the first thing to bear in mind when choosing climbers or wall plants. Soils may be chalky, sandy, clay or peat. The ideal, quoted in so many books, is 'a rich medium loam', and it is true that given such a soil you can add at will lime for chalk-lovers or peat for acid-lovers and grow thereby a wide range of plants. Acid soils can be adjusted by the addition of lime but the reverse is almost impossible; even digging out beds, removing the chalk and replacing it with a peat soil will not succeed, as the soil water, chalk-laden, will seep through and destroy the effort. If you garden upon chalky soil accept it with good grace and rejoice in the lovely plants it grows so well. Clematis will grow superbly.

When preparing the soil for climbers, remember that it is hoped that they will be permanent, so preparations should be thorough. Dig the ground deeply; against house walls you may encounter foundations, and as there is little point in planting in shallow soil you may have to plant a little way away from the wall base. Work in plenty of humus as you dig, preferably cow or farmyard manure with not too much straw. Failing this, well-rotted compost, spent hops or mushroom bed compost will do, but remember that the latter may contain a certain amount of lime. After digging but prior to planting, fork into the top 6 in (15 cm) of soil bonemeal or hoof and horn at 5 oz (170 g) per square yard (m²).

24

# Planting

Unless the ground is heavy clay, tread the soil lightly before planting. Climbers, like most shrubs, are best planted in the autumn, October to December, failing this in the spring, March to the end of April. Much may depend on the availability of the plants one is seeking. It is always best to order from nurseries in good time; nurserymen aim to grow a fairly standardised product, but nature rarely co-operates fully, and inevitably the best are taken or lifted first and go to the customer whose order is pending. If you order at the end of the planting season you may receive a less than standard plant or find the item sold out. Most nurseries sell plants in containers, which makes for easier planting and establishment and is less restrictive as regards planting dates.

Planting is a reasonably simple operation. Remove the plant from the container or root-wrap, and then dig out a hole sufficiently large to receive the root ball so that when well firmed the mark on the plant collar of the level of the nursery soil is at or only slightly below the soil surface of the border. Make sure the root ball is moist; if in doubt immerse in a bucket of water for a few minutes. Never plant into dry soil. If necessary, thoroughly flood the planting hole, leave it to percolate the surrounding ground and then plant. In humanity it is the very young and the very old who need special care, and so it is with plants. Always make sure that plants are not allowed to dry out in their early years. Apart from watering this may entail temporary shelter from drying winds. Protection from frost may also be necessary even though the same plants when older would withstand frost perfectly well. A combination of frost and drying winds can kill young evergreen plants by a 'drought' effect; if soil-water is frozen the roots are unable to absorb moisture, but the drying wind, particularly if combined with sunshine, induces transpiration and loss of water from the leaves. The best protection against frost is dry bracken, leaves, straw or even the dead stems of herbaceous plants loosely spread to about 1 ft (30 cm) thick about the base of the plant and over the immediate soil.

After planting it is often necessary to 'lead' the plant to the wall by means of a stake or cane; this should be set in the planting hole, fixed to the wall and the plant planted to the cane,

25

rather than by thrusting the cane in after planting. When planting climbers that are to ascend trees it is rarely possible to set the plant immediately against the trunk, as there is usually so much existing root present even in the case of a dead tree that successful growth is unlikely. The best method is to drive in a stake some 6 ft (1.8 m) or more from the trunk and attach it to one of the lower branches. Plant the climber against the stake where it will be free from competition from the tree roots and train it up and into the tree.

# Training

A few plants, ivy and Virginia creeper for example, are self-clinging. The vast majority, however, need support, and the effectiveness of this will play a large part in the establishment of well-grown and floriferous plants.

For plants on walls the type of fixing may depend on the degree of maintenance the wall itself will require. For walls of plain brick the fixings can be permanent and are best provided by means of screw-eyes driven into the wall in vertical lines a foot or 18 in (30–45 cm) apart and protruding 2 to 3 in (5–8 cm) from the wall. For a wall 8 ft (2.4 m) high one will require a top and bottom eye and two 'steadying' eyes in between (*see* Fig. 2). Galvanised wire (Gauge 12 or 14) is fixed to the top eye, threaded through the intermediate eyes, pulled tight and fixed to the bottom eye. Strainers are not needed for vertical wires since the

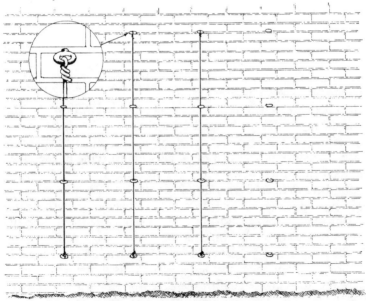

*Fig. 2   A method of fixing plants onto a brick wall.*

downward pull of the foliage keeps the wire taut.

Painted stucco walls and whitened rough cast walls present a greater problem. Sooner or later repainting becomes necessary and difficulties can arise. Flexible climbers, such as rambler roses, clematis, *Passiflora, Jasminum* etc, can be affixed in such a way as to be lowered, with care, away from the wall for painting operations. This can be achieved by fixing the wires in horizontal lines 18 in (45 cm) apart with hook and eye at one end and strainer at the other; by this means the wires can be slackened and detached, starting with the top wire, and the whole 'mat' of climber gradually laid down to the ground. Because it is not possible to use intermediate screw-eyes the maximum distance between hook and strainer should not exceed 12 ft (3.5 m); a greater length than this will cause the wire to sag, however taut the wire is made initially.

Another system involves the construction of a framework of preservative proofed wood lathes, $\frac{3}{8} \times 1$ in (10 × 25 mm) or similar dimensions, nailed so as to provide a series of squares about 18 in (45 cm) each way. The top and bottom bars may be of slightly stouter wood. The whole is suspended by stout hooks at eaves level so as to hang about 3 in (8 cm) from the wall and attached by flexible means, wire for example, to hooks at the wall base; it can then be unhooked at the top and the whole laid to the ground. Climbers or wall plants that make a stiff woody stem, *Pyracantha, Ceanothus* and wisteria for example, cannot be bent away from the wall, and one must either paint around them or give up all ideas of a painted wall.

It is possible to nail woody climbers individually to walls using nails made for this purpose. This makes more work as training proceeds, and in time can create a pockmarked effect in the brickwork. Evidence of this can often be seen on some of the lovely old kitchen garden walls of our stately homes.

Climbers over arbours will not need such elaborate means of training. The aim usually is to provide a mass of growth encompassing the building, and the type of plant used can be relied upon to climb upon its own previous growth as in nature. When climbers are planted to cover or climb through trees it is rarely possible to plant them to the tree trunk; as described on p. 26 they should be planted a little distance from the trunk and led by means of a stake into the lower branches of the tree.

28

# Pruning

Recommendations for pruning where necessary and its timing are included with the plant descriptions, but the following general observations may be worthwhile.

Always use good, sharp secateurs that cut without tearing or bruising and always cut just above a node (*see* Fig. 3). When cutting out older wood, 1 in (2.5 cm) and above, it will be necessary to use a pruning saw. These cuts should be made immediately above nodes or branch junctions. Avoid leaving snags or short stubs, which look ugly, will often die back and may cause disease. The rough surfaces left by saw cuts should be pared over with a sharp knife particularly at the cambium (bark) edge (*see*

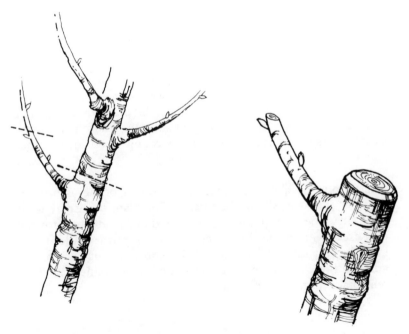

*Fig. 3 Left: before pruning, showing where cuts should be made.*
*Right: after pruning, when the cuts should be smoothed off and painted with a wound paint.*

Fig. 3) and the surface painted with a proprietary wound paint — an old recommendation was to paint with 'Stockholm tar', but I very much doubt if this can be obtained nowadays.

The reasons for pruning climbers and wall plants can be summarised as follows.

1) Some pruning may be necessary initially whilst a plant is being trained to cover a specific area. When any stem or branch is cut the topmost bud left will almost invariably be the bud that 'breaks' and produces next year's shoot. Consequently a stem or branch that is growing away from the part of a wall that it should cover can be pruned back to a suitably positioned bud which will break and produce a shoot to cover the area required.
2) Pruning may be essential in situations where a plant is outgrowing its position, encroaching unduly upon its neighbours or indeed over windows or doorways. Here again care should be taken to cut back to suitably positioned buds.
3) Cutting out dead or sickly branches may serve to revitalise an old or unthrifty plant. With this may be included the pruning out of diseased wood.
4) Pruning may encourage flowering. Some plants will give a greater display of flower by judicious pruning at the right time. In general, climbers that flower between January and May do so on wood that grew away the previous spring and ripened through the summer and autumn. Those that flower from May onwards flower on the young wood formed that spring.

Apart from the above instances it is best to prune as little as possible. The aim should be to allow the plant to display itself naturally. The climbing plants suggested as suitable for growing over trees will not need pruning (an exercise that would in any event be very difficult), but if such a climber, having over-run its arboreal host, reaches out to climb into a more valued tree firm remedial action must be taken.

# Mulching and Feeding

In nature fallen leaves provide a natural mulch. Casual examination beneath trees will reveal annual layers of dead leaves, the lowermost well rotted and permeated with surface roots of the tree. Such a mulch protects from the hard frosts of winter and conserves moisture in summer. Under garden conditions and for newly-planted material, such a mulch will need to be created. The necessity for mulching, however, will depend very much on the situation. Climbers with a free root run such as those on dead trees or on walls backing wide borders with provision for ample root run may not require mulching or feeding unless the soil is particularly poor. Ivies and Virginia creeper certainly do not need feeding once they are established, a fact borne out by the attractive coverage carried by some ancient pubs where paved courtyards extend to the very feet of the plants.

Where the border is narrow or the soil poor, annual mulching is recommended. For this purpose it is useful to have a 'leaf bin' or heap to contain the gatherings of autumn leaves. These should be stacked, turned once if possible and applied the following autumn as a light mulch. Usually feeding is not needed, but for climbers or wall plants that appear unthrifty well-rotted farm-yard manure may be added to the mulch. In spring a light dressing of a proprietary garden fertiliser may be given at the rates recommended by the manufacturer; alternatively mix together two parts by weight of superphosphate, one part sulphate of potash and two parts of sulphate of ammonia, spread thinly at 3 to 5 oz (80–140 g) per square yard (m²) and lightly fork into the top soil or into the remains of the autumn mulch.

# Pests and Diseases

Climbers and wall plants are neither more nor less prone to pest and disease attack than plants in the open, except that the sheltered wall conditions affording protection for plants also enable certain pests to overwinter in a degree of comfort that assists their multiplication.

Regular observation of one's plants should reveal any sign of leaf damage or poor growth, and the cause should then be sought. In any attack by pest or disease it is vital to identify correctly the culprit. Chemicals that may control fungus diseases are usually useless against insects, and in any case there are two types of insect pest. Firstly, there are those that destroy leaves by chewing lumps out of them; for these it is sufficient to spray the leaf surface so that they chew poison as well. Secondly, there are those that feed by inserting a fine suction tube into the leaf, drawing up and consuming the plant's sap; for these one must hit the body of the insect with chemical or, and this can be done with ornamental plants, poison the plant's sap by using a 'systemic' insecticide so that the insect takes a poisoned draught.

From this it will be seen that the identification of the cause of the trouble is very important. The brief notes given here on the more common problems may help, but if in doubt there are various agencies to whom both amateur and professional gardeners can turn for advice. Members of the Royal Horticultural Society, in return for what is still a very modest annual membership fee, have at their disposal an unrivalled pest and disease identification service. Most County Councils in Britain maintain a system of horticultural advice, sometimes provided by the Parks Departments of their larger towns. Local horticultural societies are often a pool of high quality local knowledge and a few garden centres provide a similar service.

Having identified the trouble it is easy to obtain the remedy from a sundriesman or garden centre. There is constant research and development of remedies and a recommendation to use a particular chemical today may be outdated tomorrow. Additionally Health and Safety legislation concerning what may or may not be used changes with increasing knowledge of the newly-introduced chemicals. For these reasons I make no attempt here to suggest actual remedies, but refer the reader to the above sources.

There are other means of control. Concern about the increasing use of persistent chemicals has led to considerable research in biological control where the pest is preyed upon or parasitised by some other form of life. This is by no means new; the birds foraging for insects as the gardener digs are a prime example of biological control and a striking argument for the preservation and encouragement of bird life. Another well-known friend of the gardener is the common ladybird, of which the larval stage as well as the adult feeds voraciously upon all forms of aphids, the green and black fly so pestilential upon roses and many plants. Everyone is familiar with the adult ladybird, but the larval and pupal stages are less well-known and are often taken for some exotic insect such as the notorious Colorado Beetle. The larva is black with slight red spots, about $\frac{3}{8}$ in (10 mm) long, with six legs, and is active. The pupae look like hunched-up larvae, attach themselves to leaves and gradually metamorphose into the familiar ladybird.

There are more sophisticated forms of biological control such as the minute insect (*Encarsia formosa*) introduced to parasitise the young scale stages of the troublesome greenhouse white fly. A similarly small predator (*Phytoseiulus persimilis*) of the red spider mite is recently available, and is reasonably successful under glass and in the open, particularly for wall plants. A more recent development involves a bacteria (*Bacillus thuringiensis*) sprayed in solution onto plants and thereby onto the caterpillars infesting them, the bacteria infecting and killing the caterpillars. Considerable research goes on into these forms of control that may reduce the use of possibly dangerous chemicals, but in the UK they will be of most value for crops under glass. The breeding of pest-resistant varieties is another form of protection important for food crops where the use of chemicals can cause hazards. In the case of climbers and wall plants there is no such problem, and with care in application one can rely on reasonable chemical control and the encouragement of birds and ladybirds.

The following brief notes cover some common pests and

33

diseases of climbers and wall plants in Britain, but there are a number that make an occasional appearance, some sufficiently rare to excite the enthusiasm of plant pathologists. Often the first sign of attack by sucking pests, such as aphids or scale insects, is a black sooty mould on the surface of leaves. This is not a disease in its own right but a mould growth upon the sticky secretions of these insects. So if you see sooty mould, look for the real culprit, usually on the shoots or underneath leaves above the mould.

## Pests

### Rose Aphid (*Macrosiphum rosae*)
The greenfly seen on roses from May onwards, well-known and universally troublesome.

### Woolly Aphid (*Eriosoma lanigerum*)
Purple-brown aphids covered with waxy protective wool. Sucking insects, they infest branches and often congregate on young shoots, wounds or pruning cuts. Can be troublesome on *Chaenomeles, Cotoneaster* and *Pyracantha*.

### Brown Scale (*Parthenolecanium corni*)
The most common scale, chestnut-brown, oval, convex, about $\frac{1}{4}$ in (6 mm) long. The hard scale shields the young 'crawlers' which emerge, spread to other shoots and then settle down to suck and breed. *Carpentaria, Ceanothus, Chaenomeles, Cotoneaster, Lonicera, Magnolia, Pyracantha, Rosa* and *Wisteria* can all become infested.

### Mussel Scale (*Lepidosaphes ulmi*)
Similar in life style and hosts to Brown Scale but mussel-shaped, greyish-brown in colour and about $\frac{1}{8}$ in (3 mm) long.

### Scurfy Scale (*Aulacaspis rosae*)
Dirty white scales, flat and round, about $\frac{1}{10}$ in (2 mm). Roses and other shrubby plants.

### Cushion Scale (*Chloropulvinaria floccifera*)
Can seriously infest camellias on walls (and elsewhere). A small

34

straw-coloured scale, but the long $\frac{1}{4}$ in (6 mm) cushion-like egg sac is easily seen on the undersides of leaves, although the first indication of its presence is often the inevitable sooty mould.

### Soft Scale (*Coccus hesperidum*)

Oval, very flat, translucent yellow-brown, $\frac{1}{6}$ in (4 mm). Will infest *Camellia, Clematis, Hedera, Passiflora* and in general softer-leaved plants than some of the other scales.

### Glasshouse Red Spider (*Tetranychus urticae*)

Sheltering walls and hot dry weather can produce severe infestations of this pest, the 'two-spotted mite' of American gardens, on a wide range of climbing and wall plants. The globular, eight-legged, yellow-brown mites ('red' only in the winter stages) infest the undersides of leaves; they are just visible to the naked eye. If leaves are seen to have pale yellow speckling of the upper surface, take a hand-lens and examine the undersides; if the cause is red spider it will be seen there.

## Diseases

The possibilities of diseases on climbing and wall plants are, happily, less numerous than those of pests, and are mainly as follows.

### Honey Fungus (*Armillariella mellea*)

'Bootlace Fungus' or the 'Shoestring Root Rot' of American gardens. The complete collapse and death of a tree or shrub or large parts of it is unusual and when seen the cause is often Honey Fungus. This is a saprophytic disease living in the soil on dead woody matter but prone to becoming actively parasitic on tree or shrub roots. The fruiting or visible stage is seen as a cluster of honey-coloured toadstools at the base of what by then is usually a dead tree. The term 'Bootlace Fungus' describes its underground aspect, long rhizomorphs of compressed fungal tissue resembling leather bootlaces. These grow through the soil and adhere to dead wood tissue or living roots; on the latter fungal mycelium or growth spreads up into the cambium layer of the plant choking it and causing collapse and death. It is rarely

35

seen in gardens created upon what one might term 'open' land, but is more likely in gardens adjacent to woodland or near hedgerows particularly where trees have been felled in the past and dead stumps remain. There is no reasonable cure and one must usually be resigned to the loss of the affected tree or shrub. Before replanting it is wise to fork out all 'bootlaces' and to sterilise the soil by chemical means. If possible fallow the area for a few years by growing only herbaceous or annual plants.

**Fireblight Disease (*Erwinia amylovora*)**
This is a bacterial disease affecting the pome fruit section (Pomoideae) of the rose (Rosaceae) family which includes *Cotoneaster, Crataegus, Malus, Pyracantha, Pyrus, Sorbus* and *Stransvesia*. Because of its destructive effects on pear trees it is in Britain a notifiable disease; any suspected case should be reported to the local office of the Ministry of Agriculture who publish an excellent leaflet on the disease.

The only climbing or wall plants involved are *Pyracantha* and *Cotoneaster*. In the latter genus it does not affect the small-leaved species, but attacks on larger-leaved kinds, particularly *C. salicifolia*, can be dramatic. The disease is spread by bees attracted by the sticky bacterial exudation from scars of previous years' infections. Bacteria adhere to the bees and in the course of honey gathering are transferred to the flowers where they infect the flower truss and spread into the stem. The first sign of infection is wilting and dieback of flower trusses and young shoots. Flower trusses that have died without setting berry should be suspect; there can be other causes but Fireblight is likely. Leaves on the dying shoots turn brown, and, if the outer tissue of the stem is gently pared away, a foxy-brown staining of the cambium is seen.

There is no cure and in severe attacks it is best to grub and burn the plant. If infection is seen at an early stage spread may be checked by cutting out infected shoots to at least 18 in (45 cm) below the lowest point of infection, i.e. the foxy-brown staining. The plant should be carefully observed the following year lest the cutting out has not been sufficiently thorough or effective.

**Clematis Wilt (*Ascochyta clematidina*)**
This is the only really severe problem of clematis; the cause is not certain, but appears to be associated with the fungus

*Ascochyta clematidina.* Plants and parts of plants suddenly wilt and die for no apparent reason, the large-flowered cultivars being more susceptible than the species. There is no cure but it is unwise to destroy the plant immediately, since it will sometimes throw healthy shoots in the following year.

**Pyracantha Scab (*Fusicladium pyracanthi*)**
Similar to Apple and Pear Scab, this disfigures the berries with dark scabby spotting. *Pyracantha coccinia* 'Lalandii' is said to show resistance to the disease, and several of the newer cultivars are also claimed to be resistant.

**Rose Black Spot (*Diplocarpon rosae*)**
The well-known black spotting of leaves which may die completely in bad attacks. It is a 'clean air' disease in that it is less prevalent in town districts where the slight sulphur fumes in the air limit its spread. In this respect it is similar to Hollyhock Rust which is rarely seen in towns. Black Spot seldom attacks ramblers but some other climbing roses are susceptible. Hygiene in the collecting and burning of leaves in autumn and regular fungicidal spraying in spring and summer will minimise the trouble.

**Rose Mildew (*Sphaerotheca pannosa*)**
A universal menace, this too can be controlled by regular fungicidal spraying. Some cultivars, 'Dorothy Perkins' for example, are notoriously susceptible; others such as 'Alberic Barbier' and 'Dortmund' are fairly resistant.

# Propagation

Most people when planting climbers and wall plants will pur-
chase the plants from nurseries or garden centres and have no
need or urge to propagate from them; occasionally, however,
situations may arise where it is necessary to propagate a particular plant to ensure that a replacement is to hand should it die,
or maybe to give or exchange with friends or to increase an
existing planting. In the descriptive notes brief mention is made
of propagation methods and the following is a summary of the
propagation techniques quoted there.

## Seed

Generally seeds of plant species give rise to offspring identical to
the parent plant but they will not usually perpetuate the cultivar
forms selected by man. Seed of a hybrid plant such as the rose
'Mermaid' cannot be relied upon to yield plants of 'Mermaid';
the progeny will be mixed mostly of the parents of the hybrid.

Seeds are best sown in a cold frame or glasshouse where protection from mice etc can be afforded. Small quantities are best
sown in pots or pans using John Innes seed compost; this
partially sterilised material ensures weed freedom, an important
point since shrub seeds often take a long time to germinate
during which the weed seeds in ordinary soil would overtake and
crowd out the slower shrub seedlings. The seeds should be
covered with only their own depth of compost. Very fine seeds
may be sown on the surface of the compost and covered with a
light sifting of fine sand. Some shrub seeds, *Cotoneaster* and
*Pyracantha* for example, germinate the better after exposure to
frost. This is best achieved by mixing the seed with moist sand,
putting the mixture in plastic pots (earthenware tends to crack)
plunged in a shady north-facing bed. The pots are lifted in spring
and the contents sown in the usual way. This process serves to
break the dormancy of the seeds which if they have been dried
and packeted can be difficult to break in the normal way.

38

# Division

Plants with a tuft-like habit or a creeping rootstock can be propagated in this way. It is best done during early spring when growth is starting. The plant may need to be lifted, pulled apart and the rooted underground stems transplanted into a nursery bed for growing on as individual plants. Often, however, as in the case of *Kerria japonica*, the rooted stems can be cut away from just beneath the soil surface without disturbing the plant.

# Hardwood Cuttings

Rambling roses typify plants that may be propagated by this method. Cuttings 9 to 12 in (22 to 30 cm) long of wood ripened during the current year are taken in autumn. They are made with a 'heel' of the previous year's wood neatly trimmed with a sharp knife and inserted in a bed of sandy soil in a shady place. The bed should be trodden firm and a narrow slit made by cutting perpendicularly with a spade. A little sharp sand is run into the slit before the cuttings are inserted about 4 in (10 cm) apart at half to two-thirds of their length and made very firm by treading against the slit wall. Watering may be necessary if the bed dries out and the cuttings should be kept free of weeds and aphids. Top growth will start in the spring and in the autumn the rooted cuttings may be moved to grow on with more space for a further season.

# Softwood Cuttings

As the name implies these are made from leafy shoots of the current year's growth of half-ripened wood. They should be about 3 in (8 cm) long, cut cleanly off with a sharp knife just below a node and the lower leaves removed. The prepared cuttings are then inserted up to the leaf base in pots of sandy compost and placed in a propagating frame. If this is within a greenhouse so much the better, as a moist warm atmosphere will encourage quick rooting. The frame will need to be shaded from sunlight; newspaper is useful since it can be gradually removed as the cuttings root. By this time the frames should be gradually ventilated and the young plants hardened. After a week or so they can be potted into small $3\frac{1}{2}$ in (9 cm) pots using John Innes potting compost or a proprietary sand/peat compost and kept close and humid for a few days whilst the roots establish in the new soil. The newly-potted material should be overwintered in a cold frame then planted in a nursery bed to grow on.

## Layering

This is an old method of propagation useful for certain woody subjects that are not easy to propagate by cuttings. For the amateur it is an easy method that does not require space or equipment. First a pliable branch is bent down to soil level and a notch cut in the underside. It is then pegged firmly down into the soil so that the notched portion is some 6 in (15 cm) below ground level, the depth ensuring that the stem remains moist. If the branch will not descend sufficiently, soil may be mounded up around the plant; on heavy wet land it is a good plan to supple-

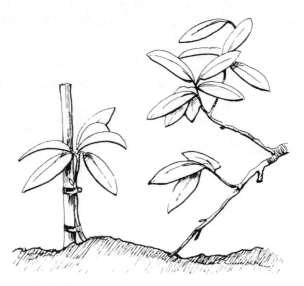

*Fig. 4 How to support a layered shoot with a small stake.*

ment the natural soil by a sandy compost. The tip of the layered shoot should be supported by a small stake (*see* Fig. 4). After rooting has taken place the layer is severed from the parent plant and in spring transplanted into a nursery bed to grow on for a year. With some subjects rooting may take a year or eighteen months. Clematis and one or two soft-stemmed subjects can be layered directly into pots of suitable sandy compost sunk into the soil.

## Grafting and Budding

These require knowledge and experience and are of course standard practice on nurseries for certain plants. When undertaken by amateurs it is usually because of interest in the practice, the principles of which are briefly as follows. A stem portion, the scion, is grafted onto a young plant, the stock, of a kind that is easy to grow and compatible, i.e. of the same family and known from experience to be receptive. Thus the 'Corkscrew' Hazel, *Corylus avellana* 'Contorta', whose twisted habit does not come true from seed and which is difficult to root by cuttings, is grafted onto seedlings of the common Hazel. Budding, as the name implies, is the insertion of a leaf-bud of the chosen cultivar into the stem of a stronger and more easily grown stock. It is the universal method of producing bush and standard roses (and some climbers) as well as walnuts, ornamental maples and various other subjects. Anyone needing or wishing to graft or bud plant material should consult that fine classic on the subject, *The Grafter's Handbook* by R. J. Garner (5th edition, Cassell, 1989).

# Descriptive List of Genera

Numbers in brackets refer to colour plates.

## *Abelia* (Caprifoliaceae)

Flowering from July to October. Planted where they like to be planted; at the base of a south or west wall *Abelias* in shades of white or pink attract bees anxiously garnering the last of summer's honey. A plant that seems evocative of drowsy late summer afternoons.

Two kinds are attractive, amenable wall plants and a third well worth a try by those in milder counties. The first, *A. schumannii*, from Central China, was introduced in 1910 by 'Chinese Wilson', E. H. Wilson (1876–1930), the Warwickshire garden-boy who went on to become the celebrated plant collector of over 1,000 new plant introductions and finally Director of the internationally famous Arnold Arboretum in America. This *Abelia*, growing to 3 or 4 ft (1 to 1.25 m) has red-brown slightly arching downy stems and small light green leaves from whose axils are borne in twos and threes rosy-pink bell-shaped flowers.

The second is *A. x grandiflora*, taller than the first and with arching stems, having glossy dark green leaves and terminating in heads of short twigs each with two to five sepalled light brown calyces. These are attractive and persistent and with the shrub's vigour and productive growth a useful source of flower arranger's material. The plant is a hybrid between *A. chinensis* and *A. uniflora*, raised in Rovellii Nurseries, Pallanza near Lake Maggiore in 1886. A recent variation of great merit is *A. x grandiflora* 'Frances Mason', equally floriferous but with the rich green foliage gaily variegated with yellow.

The third member, *A. floribunda*, is much more tender and was introduced from Mexico in 1841. In the milder counties of Britain it will do well on a south wall displaying its 2 in (5 cm) long rosy-red, pendulous, funnel-shaped flowers backed by glossy evergreen leaves. The most attractive of all and worth trying in favoured areas.

*Abelia x grandiflora* and *A. schumannii* are Zone 5 plants in the

USA; *A. floribunda* is Zone 7. Propagation is by cuttings of semi-ripe wood struck in gentle heat. Prune only to keep within bounds cutting out, preferably older wood, in spring.

## *Abeliophyllum distichum* (Oleaceae)

Early in the alphabet of shrubs and early to flower, easily grown yet so seldom seen as to deserve the epithet 'rare'. It is a close relative of the *Forsythia* and probably the nearest we are likely to get to a 'white' *Forsythia*. The delicately-scented white flowers are small, four-petalled with soft yellow stamens and crowded on the bare twigs. They would be insignificant in the full flood of summer flowers, but on a cold drear February day are welcome and encouraging.

A comparative newcomer to gardens, it was collected by Prof. T. Nakai in the Chinsen Hills in Middle Korea in 1919 and introduced to Britain in 1932. The only species of the genus, its distribution was confined to a very small area, and had it not been collected and propagated in gardens it could well have become extinct, particularly with the devastation in Korea in recent times.

It appears hardy enough in Britain but flowers better after a hot summer and merits a place on a south wall. Korean winters are colder and their summers hotter than those of Britain, so it is likely that it would do well in many areas of the United States. It is rather slow-growing but not particular as to soil, flowering on both old wood and that of the previous year's growth. Pruning should be confined to cutting out only dead or very weak wood. Propagation is by summer cuttings of half-ripened wood in a close frame.

## *Abutilon* (Malvaceae)

Attractive shrubs with showy hollyhock-like flowers. The name is derived from the Arabic word for a species of mallow. In most areas of Britain they need the shelter of a wall to give of their best. In Victorian times many variously coloured tender varieties were grown but these have mostly disappeared; one persists, the

43

variegated leaved *A. striatum* 'Thompsonii', which is still frequently used in summer bedding displays and is an example of transmissible virus leaf variegation. A shoot of the variety grafted upon a green-leaved stock will transmit the variegation to the stock, an example of virus infection put to good use. The following species and hybrids are those most likely to succeed in Britain and by the attractiveness of their flowers will amply repay the possibility of loss in unusually severe winters. They are Zone 8 plants in the USA.

### *A. megapotamicum* (2)

The name means 'big river' and refers to the plant's Brazilian origin. Introduced from the Rio Grande in 1864 the light green acuminate leaves make a pleasing background to the pendulous flowers whose balloon-like red calyces with contrasting yellow petals and central boss of chocolate-coloured stamens invariably attract the eye. An excellent low shrub for south-facing walls, in such a situation it will flower steadily from mid-May to autumn. Young plants are susceptible to frost damage and should be protected with a mulch of bracken or similar covering. Pruning is not necessary, but the plant's appearance and flower display are improved if the main leading shoots can be tied in to wires or lattice against the wall. Very occasionally the plant may be sold or labelled as *A. vexillarium*, this being the name first given when it was introduced and under which it was illustrated in *Curtis's Botanical Magazine* (t.5717).

### *A. ochsenii* (1)

Although first described as long ago as 1856 under the name *Anoda ochsenii* from Valdivia in Chile, this plant was not cultivated in British gardens until 1957, when Mr E. B. Anderson raised plants from seed sent from Chile. At present it is seldom seen outside botanic gardens. The plant lacks the dense tomentum on stems and leaves of *A. vitifolium* and appears greener in consequence. In habit it is like *A. vitifolium* and will attain 6 to 10 ft (1.8 to 3m) in Britain. The flowers are borne singly or in pairs, as opposed to those of *A. vitifolium* which are borne three or four together, and are smaller but of a bright mauve. Although probably hardier than *A. vitifolium* it is best placed in a similar situation and given similar treatment.

## A. x suntense

This hybrid between *A. vitifolium* and *A. ochsenii* can be recommended as being better than either parent and probably hardier. It bears in profusion typical hollyhock-type flowers of clear purple-violet on the current year's shoots in May and June. The plant came to notice when exhibited at the Royal Horticultural Society's show in June 1969 by Mr Geoffrey Gorer of Sunte House in Sussex. It arose in a batch of seedlings from a site where *A. vitifolium* and *A. ochsenii* grew together; it was described in the *RHS Journal* for 1971 (p. 274) and is figured at t.679 (New Series) in *Curtis's Botanical Magazine* (1974). A deliberate cross between *A. vitifolium* and *A. ochsenii* was made by Messrs Hilliers of Winchester and the resulting hybrid named 'Jermyns', under which name the plant may sometimes be seen. Mr Gorer's plant was, however, the first to be described, and *A. x suntense* is the correct and accepted name. Like its parents no pruning is needed and like them it thrives in a sheltered south or west-facing wall angle or recess.

## A. vitifolium (3)

Introduced in 1836 by 'Capt. Cottingham, a zealous horticulturist', who received seed from Chile, this plant has been long and fairly widely grown in Britain. In a suitably sheltered situation it grows vigorously making an upright soft-wooded shrub with a dense tomentum over leaves and stems. The cultivar 'Veronica Tennant' has slightly larger flowers of good mauve colour, is free-flowering and the better plant to grow. There is a good white form 'Tennant's White', having an attractive slightly pleated texture to the flowers; if obtainable this is better than the more frequently listed 'Album'.

## Acacia (Leguminosae)

The lovely 'Mimosa' that is imported from the South of France to cheer February's days with colour and fragrance is a plant worth trying in the south and south-west and in areas favoured by the warming influence of the Gulf Stream. Even in these areas the additional protection of a south-facing wall is desirable for warmth and protection from wind; it is a 'risk' plant in Britain and any USA Zone below 8, but a risk well worth taking.

Of the vast number of *Acacia* species, *A. dealbata*, the 'Mimosa' or 'Silver Wattle', is the hardiest and most likely to succeed. It forms a tree with attractive silvery grey-green leaves and bears in early spring panicles of yellow, fragrant flowers that individually resemble minute powder-puffs and are totally unlike the typical pea flowers associated with the family Leguminosae.

Propagated from seed and available from specialist nurserymen it can achieve considerable height and requires therefore to be planted against nothing less than a two-storey building or wall of that height. It requires no pruning but should be tied to the wall at intervals to prevent wind damage. A native of New South Wales and Tasmania, it was introduced in 1820. It is not very lime tolerant and flowers better after hot summers that have ripened the flowering wood.

Other species can be tried. *A. longifolia*, the 'Sidney Golden Wattle', is slightly more tolerant of lime, the flowers more like small bushy 'tails' than powder-puffs; it is used as a street tree in California. *A. pycnantha* and *A. riceana* have both been grown successfully in the warmer parts of Britain and if obtainable are well worth a try.

## *Actinidia* (Actinidiaceae)

Three species of *Actinidia* are commonly grown in British gardens; two of these, *A. arguta* and *A. chinensis*, are very vigorous large-leaved climbers suitable for climbing over derelict trees or to clothe large areas of high wall or to associate on walls or pergolas with large buildings or landscape areas. The third, *A. kolomikta*, is a slender, far more gentle soul, barely achieving more than 8 ft (2.4 m) on the west-facing walls which suit it so well.

*Actinidia arguta*, the most vigorous of the three, is a native of China, Japan and the Amur region. The dark lustrous green leaves are some 5 to 8 in (12 to 20 cm) long and as much broad. The fragrant white flowers are small and not a significant feature.

*Actinidia chinensis* is slightly less vigorous and supplies the 'Chinese Gooseberries' more recently known as 'Kiwi Fruit' due to their intensive production in New Zealand where considerable work has been done on improved fruiting clones. For our purpose *A. chinensis* differs in that stems and leaves are set with decorative brown stiff hairs. The white to buff flowers are large, $1\frac{1}{2}$ in (3 cm) across but still not a feature. First noted by Robert Fortune in China in 1847 but not introduced to Britain until 1900; quite hardy and sometimes sets fruit here.

Totally different is *A. kolomikta* (**4**), a slender climber grown solely for the beauty of its 3 to 6 in (7 to 15 cm) leaves which often have up to half the leaf coloured white or pink or indeed both. The foliage is most striking in early summer; a position in the sun is necessary to bring out the colour and it does best on a west wall. Native of Manchuria, China and Japan it is completely hardy in Britain and down to Zone 5 in USA. Introduced from Japan in 1877 by Charles Maries, who called it the 'cat plant' in reference to the almost incredible attraction the leaves and stems have for cats, an attraction so great that it is sometimes necessary to surround young plants with wire to keep off feline intruders who paw and drool over the plants.

## *Akebia* (Lardizabalaceae)

If one had to sum up *A. quinata*, the most commonly-grown species of this genus, in one word it would be 'coverage'. For this it is superb and in the USA, where it is a Zone 5 plant, horticulturists write caveats as to its invasiveness. These are not necessary in Britain but it is fair to say that its best position is to clothe a worn out tree or an unsightly shed. In Britain it is evergreen only in mild winters and loses its leaves when conditions are severe.

The specific name *quinata* refers of course to the five-lobed slender-stalked leaves, which are of a soft pleasing green and set on stems that will twine around any support. The chocolate-purple flowers are insignificant but carry a spicy fragrance; only rarely are they followed by the very distinctive grey purple 3–4 in (8–10 cm) long sausage-like fruits. This failure to produce fruit also occurs in America where hand pollination has been shown to produce fruits readily. Flowering as it does in April it seems likely that a mild spring and hot summer may be necessary for fruit production. *Akebia quinata* was introduced by Robert Fortune from China in 1845. Another species, *A. trifoliata*, deciduous and with three-lobed leaves but otherwise very similar to *A. quinata*, was introduced from the same area in 1895. Propagated by summer stem cuttings or by root cuttings or more easily by layers; both species are fairly hungry plants and need a good loam soil.

## *Ampelopsis* (Vitaceae)

The climbers constituting the genera *Ampelopsis*, *Parthenocissus*, and *Vitis* have had a botanically varied life, having at times, for taxonomic reasons, been moved from genus to genus. Thus the 'Virginia creeper', still sometimes listed as *Ampelopsis veitchii*, will now be found under *Parthenocissus*, and many *Ampelopsis* were for a long time known as *Vitis*. All the climbers that botanists have retained as *Ampelopsis* have curling tendrils by means of which they can, with initial support, climb into trees or cover pergolas or fences. They do not have the self-clinging characteristics necessary to cover walls without assistance. All are deciduous and Zone 5–6 plants in the USA. Of the number of species listed the following may be considered as being the most useful as well as those most likely to be available.

### *A. aconitifolia*
A luxurious-looking and hardy plant, with five leafleted leaves which are finely and deeply divided, giving the whole plant an airy, ferny appearance. After a hot summer, bunches of small, orange-yellow fruits are produced. A native of North China introduced around 1868.

### *A. brevipedunculata*
A vigorous plant often listed as *Ampelopsis heterophylla*. The five-lobed cordate leaves are not unlike those of the hop plant. Following hot summers, masses of small porcelain blue fruits are produced. Introduced from North Asia around 1870.

### *A. brevipedunculata* 'Elegans'
This form, which has green leaves variegated white and pink, is often listed as *A. heterophylla* 'Tricolor' or 'Variegata'. Much weaker growing than the type, it is suitable for patio walls where it will need the assistance of wires or trellis to climb but will

48

provide very attractive cover. A north or east aspect is best since the variegated leaves do not take kindly to hot sun.

### A. chaffanjonii

Previously known as *Vitis watsoniana*, it has large pinnate leaves up to a foot (30 cm) in length. A fine plant to grow into a tree, the glossy green leaves being purple beneath are effective when seen from the ground. Discovered in Central China by E. H. Wilson (1876–1930) in 1900, it colours magnificently in autumn.

### A. megalophylla

Previously *Vitis megalophylla*, this is a slow-growing plant with massive pinnate leaves up to 2 ft (60 cm) long — hence the specific name from the Greek, *mega* meaning 'great' and *phyll* meaning 'leaf'. Suited only for climbing into large trees where it will reach 30 or 40 ft (9–12 m). Very impressive in the right situation; it occasionally bears loose bunches of purplish fruit. Introduced from Western China in 1894.

### A. orientalis

A much weaker climber than either of the foregoing, and suited to scramble over or through shrubs of possibly no great value. Leaves pinnate with 3 in (7.5 cm) leaflets. In hot summers it will produce bunches of redcurrant-like fruits. Introduced from Asia Minor around 1818.

*Ampelopsis* are easily propagated by means of leafy cuttings of half-ripened growth taken in July–August and inserted in sand in a cold frame.

## *Araujia* (Asclepiadaceae)

The 'Cruel Plant', *A. sericofera*, can be grown outside only in the mildest parts of Britain and then only against the protection of a wall. It is a twining, vigorous, evergreen climber with pale green leaves that are slightly felted beneath. The salver-shaped white flowers are slightly fragrant. It gets its curious common name from the fact that in its native South America it is pollinated by night-flying moths whose long proboscides often become entrapped by the glutinous pollen adhering to them. In the early day the sun shines on the pollen drying it thus enabling the moth to release itself.

Introduced by J. Tweedie (1775–1862) from Buenos Aires in 1830, the plant likes a good loamy soil and flowers freely enough in the Channel Islands and places of similar climate. It has also survived and flowered in Surrey. It is doubtless a Zone 9 plant in the USA. Propagated by seeds or by cuttings of ripe wood inserted in sand in heat in late autumn.

## *Aristolochia* (Aristolochiaceae)

Not in any way showy or decorative are the half-dozen 'Birthworts' that are hardy in Britain. The flowers, however, are interesting: there is no corolla but the tubular calyx is bent in a curious fashion so as to resemble a Dutch smoking pipe, hence the other common name 'Dutchman's Pipe'. The calyx is slightly flared at the 'Bowl' end giving an impression of a petal.

They are not widely planted and the most frequently seen, sometimes under the earlier names of *A. sipho* or *A. durior*, is *A. macrophylla*. It was accurately and beautifully figured in *Curtis's Botanical Magazine* (t.534) in 1801. The writer of the accompanying text emphasised its large cordate leaves 'of a fine dark green' and pointed out that 'the flowers are curiously formed but being concealed below the leaves are not conspicuous'. He adds that it was 'first sent over to this country by Mr John Bartram of Philadelphia about the year 1763'. There is little to add to that, except that it is happy in a lime soil and can be used to cover large areas of north wall, where it will need lattice or wire to twine around. A better use for it is to cover summer houses, pergolas or arbours. As one might assume from its native habitat, it can be planted down to Zone 4 in the USA.

My own favourite of the genus is *A. sempervirens* (5), sometimes called *A. altissima*. The plant is suitable for the smaller garden and most importantly the flowers are presented in front of the leaves appearing to the onlooker like curious little dull yellow faces. The leaves are not large, 2 to 3 in (5 to 8 cm), and are dark lustrous green. This is the species hailing from the dry hillsides of Crete. It needs a south wall and light soil and may be savaged by a hard winter but is worth growing as an interesting plant.

## *Asteranthera* (Gesneriaceae)

Another of the fascinating but rather difficult plants of South America. A native of the temperate forests of Chile, *Asteranthera ovata* enjoys a moist, almost saturated, atmosphere that is not easy to find in Britain. Despite this, and although not as floriferous as in its native Chile, it has grown and flowered quite well in Sussex and in moist gardens in the west of Scotland. Probably a Zone 9 plant in the USA but only in suitable situations.

A climbing evergreen which roots readily at the nodes, its light green leaves, from $\frac{1}{2}$ to $1\frac{1}{2}$ in (1 to 4 cm) across, are roundish in outline with shallow, round indentations. The flowers are funnel-shaped with flared lobes, rich raspberry-red in colour and with a small calyx that is curiously toothed; they are borne from mid-summer onwards. The plant requires a rich leafy soil and will cling to a moist wall or over a fallen tree or wood. It propagates very easily by cuttings; consequently it could be planted as a 'risk' plant far more often than at present. It was collected and introduced by H. F. Comber (1897–1969) in 1927.

## *Azara* (Flacourtiaceae)

The name of this genus of evergreen shrubs commemorates J. N. Azara (1731–1804), a Spanish scientist. All the species are natives of Chile and Argentina and inclined to be tender; two, however, planted in the right situations, are good wall plants.

The first and most commonly planted is *A. microphylla*, introduced from Chile by Richard Pearce in 1861. A shrub or small tree rarely more than 15 ft (4.5 m) high, its specific name refers to the fact that two leaves, one large, $\frac{1}{2}$ to $\frac{3}{4}$ in (1–1.5 cm), and one much smaller, $\frac{1}{4}$ in (0.5 cm) appear to come from each node; in fact the small leaf is a stipule. The charm of the shrub lies in the vanilla fragrance of its insignificant flowers borne in profusion on the undersides of the stems. They open in February and on a mild, still winter's day the vanilla fragrance can be perceptible for some distance.

The second, *A. lanceolata*, was found by Charles Darwin in 1834 whilst on the celebrated voyage of the *Beagle*, but was not introduced until 1926 when H. F. Comber collected it in Chile.

51

The leaves are larger, 1 to 2 in (2.5 to 5 cm), than those of *A. microphylla*, but again with a leaf-like stipule at the base. The flowers, in contrast to those of *A. microphylla*, are prominent, comprising tufts of golden yellow stamens like small powder puffs, sweetly-scented and closely set on the stems. Although flowering later, in April, it is not as hardy as *A. microphylla*. It flowers well on a north or west wall that is screened from cold winds.

Both species can be propagated from cuttings in gentle heat, and pruning other than to train or restrict is not required. *Azaras* are risk plants for anywhere below Zone 8 in the USA, and require a wall in most parts of Britain.

## *Berberidopsis* (Flacourtiaceae)

The Coral Barbary or Coral Plant belongs to a monotypic genus, that is to say only one species of the genus, *B. corallina*, is known. This was introduced by Richard Pearce in 1862 from a limited forest area in Chile where it is now thought to be extinct. Fortunately this lovely evergreen scrambling climber has been a favourite of plant connoisseurs for many years, and although not widely planted is unlikely, whilst interest in gardens and good plants persists, to become extinct.

Like many Chilean shrubs it needs a deep moist soil and shade with protection from winds. Produced from the end of July until autumn the very lovely, rich-red, half-inch (13 mm), slightly fleshy flowers hang in clusters like pendent racemes of jewels against the grey-green, coarsely-toothed, elliptic-shaped leaves. On north walls, for which it is suggested, it will need some support of wire or lattice, or it can be trained to scramble into or over a shrub of little worth. Its country of origin and need for shelter make it a Zone 9 subject in the USA. No pruning — if it will ramble, let it! Propagated by summer cuttings or layers.

## *Berchemia* (Rhamnaceae)

A small genus of deciduous twining climbers with little garden appeal primarily because their chief attraction, the blue-black fruits, are rarely if ever produced in Great Britain, and the flowers are small and insignificant. Nurserymen list several species, two of which may be singled out for attention. *Berchemia giraldiana* will climb to 20 ft (6 m), producing arching shoots which take on an interesting reddish-brown colour as they age. The leaves, slightly downy beneath, have prominent parallel veins. The other, *B. racemosa*, makes a strong-growing scandent shrub rather than a climber. The leaves like those of *B. giraldiana* are quite attractive and turn a lovely soft yellow in autumn. Both species like a good moist soil and can be propagated by summer cuttings in a sand frame. Zone 7 plants in the USA, and useful climbers for the wild or woodland garden.

## *Buddleia* (Loganiaceae)

The common buddleia is familiar as an August-flowering occupant of gardens and as the shrub that sprang up and bloomed on the bombed sites of British cities in World War 2. The genus contains several slightly tender species; three of these, *B. auriculata*, *B. colvilei* and *B. crispa*, are plants of character for favourable situations and wall protection.

Virtually evergreen, *B. auriculata* has dark-green, lanceolate leaves having two auricles (ear-like protrusions) clasping the stem at the base of each pair of leaves. The beautifully fragrant creamy-white flowers, the plant's attraction, are produced from September to January. It should be pruned by having the current year's growth cut back to within two or three buds of the old wood in early spring. A South African plant introduced in 1813, it is worth surrounding the base of young plants with litter during hard weather.

*Buddleia colvilei* (6) has the typical growth we associate with the common buddleia, but is rather more lax and with a covering of red-brown 'wool' on the younger growth. The individual flowers, produced in drooping panicles during June, are large, 1 in (2.5 cm) long and of a fine red-purple colour. The showiest of the genus, it was introduced from the Himalayas in 1849. No pruning necessary other than the unlikely need to restrict its spread.

The July-flowering *Buddleia crispa* has leaves and young

53

shoots so richly covered with close white down that the lilac-coloured flowers appear to sit luxuriously in a white all-surrounding fur coat. Introduced from North India in 1850 it should be pruned as for *B. auriculata*. All three species are propagated by cuttings of late summer half-ripened wood. For the USA it may be assumed that these species are limited to Zone 8 and above. The genus honours the name of the Rev. Adam Buddle (1660–1715), an early British botanist.

## *Caesalpinia* (Leguminosae) (7)

In warm areas and against hot sunny walls the 'Poinciana', flamboyant 'Bird of Paradise' flower, and novelists' background to torrid tropical romance, is a possibility. More prosaically the plant is *C. gilliesii*, whose flowers of rich yellow, each with its cluster of scarlet stamens, are borne on erect racemes like gaudy candelabra.

More accommodating as regards our sunshine record is *C. japonica* with flowers of similar type but softer yellow and with stamens red rather than scarlet. Grown successfully in the London area, indeed there is a fine plant at Hampton Court, it was introduced from Japan by Messrs Veitch, the celebrated nineteenth-century nurserymen. Flowering in June–July it has the same long pinnate leaves as the *Poinciana*, a bright green backcloth to the striking flower spikes. The soft look of the foliage is deceptive, for the plant is armed with the most vicious spines. Pruning other than for containment is not necessary; an open well-drained soil is essential; and propagation is by seed or layers. *C. gilliesii* was introduced from the Argentine in 1829 but in Britain has succeeded in only a few favoured spots. Both species would probably grow in USA Zones 9 upwards. The generic name honours Andreas Caesalpini (1519–1603), an Italian botanist.

## *Calceolaria* (Scrophulariaceae)

The only shrubby *Calceolaria* that can be safely grown outside in Britain, *C. integrifolia* has with me survived more frost and

54

neglect than it should. Bright green leaves, slightly hairy and rather clammy to the touch, set off panicles of clear yellow, pouch-shaped flowers produced steadily from July until autumn. A plant for south- or west-facing walls, it seldom grows more than 4 ft (1.2 m) high and is well worth planting at the base of, for example, the blue-flowered *Solanum crispum* or beside, indeed perhaps separating, pink-flowered *Phygelius* and blue *Caryopteris*.

It has been grown in Britain since 1822 when it was introduced from Chile by the Horticultural Society. Not a long-lived plant but easily propagated by cuttings of the young growth taken in August–September. No pruning is required; the woody stems are distinctly brittle and care has to be taken that they are not broken off in the course of garden operations. In the USA probably a Zone 7 plant.

## *Callistemon* (Myrtaceae)

One of the 'Bottle Brushes' hardy enough to grow in Britain as a wall plant, *C. citrinus* comes from New South Wales and was introduced in 1788. In British gardens it makes a rather straggling bush about 8 ft (2.5 m) high. The very striking 'brush' is composed of numerous small flowers each with long red stamens tipped with golden anthers. Their cylindrical arrangement around the stem gives the characteristic bottle brush effect. In most plants, flowering terminates the growth of the flower-bearing shoot; this plant is unusual in that the many stems bearing flowers continue to grow in length, each bearing another 'brush' in the following and successive years.

Happy in any reasonable well-drained soil, propagation is by means of cuttings; its USA Zone limit is probably 8 with wall protection. The long narrow leaves if crushed smell faintly of lemon, hence the specific name. A species allied to *C. citrinus*, *C. subulatus* has been found to be hardier, but is not, as yet, widely available. Another species, *C. salignus* (**8**), a tree of almost 30 ft (10 m) in the wild makes in Britain a pleasant shrub of about 8 ft (2.4 m) against a wall. The profusely-produced 'brushes' are red or pale lemon in colour.

55

## *Camellia* (Theaceae)

Camellias are usually grown in light shaded woodland but can be very effective as free-standing shrubs against north or west walls or trained on the walls themselves. Although rarely grown in this fashion they can in fact be readily trained, the dark green leaves and scarlet flowers looking particularly lovely against a white wall. A suitable system of support wires is necessary and it is then merely a matter of tying in shoots as they arise. Camellias are relatively hardy but early morning sun can damage frosted buds or flowers and for this reason a north or west wall is best. They prefer peaty soil; any lime rapidly produces leaf chlorosis and it may be necessary when planting against walls, where there is often a residue of lime or mortar, to dig out the existing soil and replace with a peaty compost. Propagation is by cuttings, preferably leaf-bud cuttings, of half-ripened wood inserted in a frame in a peat-sand compost with a little bottom heat.

Camellias flourish in the southern United States where there are enthusiastic Camellia Societies, and where much work has been done as regards new varieties. Australia and New Zealand have also contributed greatly to the recent growth of interest in the genus. From the thousands of cultivars available the following are a few that are well known and reliable.

| | |
|---|---|
| 'Adolphe Audusson' | Blood-red. Semi-double. |
| 'Alba Plena' | Double white. |
| 'Apollo' | Semi-double, rose-red. |
| 'Donation' | Orchid-pink, large semi-double. |
| 'Donckelarii' | Semi-double, red marbled white. |
| 'Elegans' | Large deep peach pink. |
| 'Francis Hanger' | Single, white. |
| 'Gloire de Nantes' | Semi-double, rose-pink. |
| 'Mary Williams' | Crimson-rose, large single, vigorous. |
| 'Mathotiana' | Large double crimson. |
| 'Captain Rawes' | Double carmine-pink, hardy. |
| 'J. C. Williams' | Single phlox-pink. |

## *Campsis* (Bignoniaceae)

The genus contains two species, one from east Asia and one from the USA; both are hardy in Britain but need sun and the shelter of a south wall.

*Campsis radicans*, the American Trumpet Vine, is the hardier of the two. A deciduous climber, it clings, like ivy, by means of aerial roots. The pinnate leaves are dark green above, downy beneath. Clusters of glorious orange-scarlet trumpet-shaped flowers are produced in August and September on the ends of the current season's growth. A native of the south-east United States it was introduced to Britain, sent home presumably by settlers, as long ago as 1640.

The other species, *C. grandiflora*, was introduced from China in 1800. It is similar and even more colourful than *C. radicans* but even on a south wall does not flower well here. A cross between the two species, *C. x tagliabuana*, arose on a nursery near Milan in the mid-nineteenth century. Many forms of this were distributed by French nurserymen; the best known, and still available, is the salmon-coloured 'Madam Galen'. It is not self-clinging and requires supports around which to twine.

*Campsis* grow away rapidly but once the allotted area of wall space has been covered by a framework of stems the annual growth should be pruned back after leaf-fall to within two or three buds of the previous year's growth, as is done with grape vines. If trained on the wall of a low building it will be noticed that it is growth which extends so as to lay on the roof tiles that flowers most readily. This may be due to a greater measure of reflected heat. Propagated by cuttings or layers, *C. radicans* is, as one might expect, hardy in Zone 5 and above in the USA; *C. grandiflora* to Zone 6 only.

## *Carpenteria* (Philadelphaceae) (9)

Looking at a well-flowered plant of *C. californica*, the only species in this genus, one might assume it to be an evergreen 'Syringa'. This would be a reasonable assumption for it is closely allied to *Philadelphus*, the 'Syringa' or 'Mock Orange Blossom' of our gardens, and has a very similar flower.

An evergreen wall shrub of some 6 to 10 ft (1.8–3 m) in height

57

it needs well-drained soil and plenty of sun, preferably a warm south or west wall. The clusters of fragrant 2 to 3 in (5–7.5 cm) white flowers each with a prominent central cluster of yellow stamens are backed by bright green leaves. A native of California, and reckoned a Zone 8 plant in the USA, it was introduced to Europe around 1880. It can be raised from seed and the variability of the progeny has led to the existence of some rather poor, narrow petalled forms and possibly the neglect of what is a good plant. For this reason it is worth while to check the source and stock of purchased plants. Given a good form such as that in plate **9** it is a plant worth trying in reasonably sheltered gardens. The generic name honours Professor Carpenter, a botanist of Louisiana, USA.

## *Caryopteris* (Verbenaceae)

Wall protection is not needed for *Caryopteris* but its low shrubby habit make it a good subject to place in front of climbers whose lower stems are bare and unattractive. Furthermore it is one of the few blue-flowering shrubs, and is welcome in this respect.

Two species, *C. incana* and *C. mongolica*, both from China, have been in Britain since 1844, but it was the hybrid between the two, *C. x clandonensis* (raised in the early 1930s by the late Arthur Simmonds, a great and effective Secretary of the Royal Horticultural Society, and named after Clandon, the Surrey village where he lived), that drew attention to its value as a garden plant. Others have been introduced since, the darker 'Kew Blue' and 'Ferndown' and the American 'Heavenly Blue', more erect but the same colour as 'Arthur Simmonds', which is the correct name of the first cross although this is still often sold as 'Clandonensis'. All benefit from hard pruning in the spring and can be propagated by cuttings of half-ripened wood inserted in a sand frame. The USA limit of hardiness is Zone 8 where it is suggested that the plant be protected by a light mulch and pruned to the ground in spring.

The thoughtful gardener will find numerous uses for this shrub. Flowering in September, it associates well with either of the yellow *Clematis, C. tangutica* and *C. orientalis*, flowering at the same time. If sufficiently shrubby it can support slender

58

yellow-flowered climbers, such as *Eccremocarpus scaber* 'Aureus' or *Tropaeolum peregrinum*, and combine to make a charming picture.

## *Ceanothus* (Rhamnaceae)

Blue-flowered shrubs are not numerous so it would benefit the gardener to take full advantage of this North American genus, most of whose members are blue-flowered and needing wall shelter. There are a number of species and cultivars, evergreen and deciduous. The evergreen kinds trained to a wall normally require little pruning, and any necessary cutting back should be done immediately after flowering. They are fast-growing but not very long-lived shrubs, but fortunately are easily propagated by summer cuttings in gentle heat. The flowers are small, each about $\frac{3}{16}$ in (5 mm), but very numerous and borne in panicles or clusters. For the purpose of wall cover the evergreen kinds are preferable and the following is a representative selection for this purpose. Most of those described are from California or have Californian species as parents and may be considered Zone 7 shrubs for the USA. Any well-drained soil suits them.

### *C.* 'Burkwoodii'
Raised in the 1930s by Burkwood & Skipwith Ltd, then of Kingston-on-Thames, Surrey. This shrub will form an evergreen 5 to 6 ft (1.5 to 1.8 m) high, bearing small green leaves that are greyish beneath, the flowers rich bright blue from July to October.

### *C.* 'Delight'
The result of a cross between *C. papillosus* and *C. rigidus* made by Burkwood & Skipwith. May-flowering, it is one of the hardiest and a lovely blue.

### *C. dentatus* (10)
May-flowering and probably the most commonly planted, and extremely worth while. The small leaves are up to $\frac{1}{2}$ in (1 cm) long. Bright blue flowers in roundish clusters.

### *C. thyrsiflorus*
Also hardy, this has pale blue flowers in stalked clusters produced in May and June. Introduced from California in 1837.

59

## *C. x veitchianus*

A natural hybrid introduced by William Lobb from California in 1853. Origin uncertain, the flowers are of deep blue, borne in closely-packed heads during May and June.

## *Celastrus* (Celastraceae)

A climber that is happiest scrambling through and over a small derelict tree or one of no value. From a gardener's point of view the best, indeed the only, species to plant, is *C. orbiculatus* (11). The flowers are small and of no account, but in fruit the pea-sized berries split open to reveal vivid scarlet seeds contrasting against the yellow husks and the pale gold of the autumn leaves. On a well-grown plant these fruits hang in chains making a display that lasts several months, since birds do not appear to care for the seeds. It is a vigorous plant and requires good deep soil to give of its best. Propagated by seeds or layers, it is a native of north-east Asia, and has been an occupant of British gardens since 1870 when seeds were sent to Kew. It is hardy in Britain and in the USA down to Zone 4; in fact America has its own native 'Bittersweet', *C. scandens*, a fine climber for similar purposes there but which strangely does not fruit well in Britain.

In nature *C. orbiculatus* is dioecious, that is to say male and female flowers are carried on separate plants. In 1958 an FCC was awarded to an hermaphrodite form, a clone in which the two sexes are present on the one plant; when buying, this should be secured if at all possible. Failing that, enquire as to the sex of the plants on sale. If they are not hermaphrodite it will be essential to plant one of each if the lady is to give you the superb display you seek.

## *Cestrum* (Solanaceae) (12)

Given a sunny south wall and a reasonable climate or micro-climate it can be worth taking a gamble with *Cestrums*, natives of Central America, as wall plants. As proof one may record that plate 12 was taken in a London garden.

The one most frequently seen and probably the best of those we can grow outside in Britain is *C.* 'Newellii'. A seedling of garden origin raised by a Mr Newell of Downham Market, Norfolk, in the 1880s, the flowers are funnel-shaped, borne in clusters at the shoot ends and of a good bright red. Others worth trying by the adventurous include *C. aurantiacum*, sub-evergreen and with orange flowers; *C. elegans*, evergreen with pendent, slightly downy shoots and reddish-purple funnel-shaped flowers in hanging racemes that are produced quite readily on plants on sheltered walls in Cornwall. The deciduous *C. parqui* is hardier but less decorative; the flowers; fragrant at night, are greenish-yellow. Another species worth trying is *C. fasciculatum*, which has terminal clusters of rosy-carmine pitcher-shaped flowers. All are June-flowering.

Propagation by cuttings of half-ripened wood in gentle heat is fairly easy. Pruning is unlikely to be necessary in Britain but in severe weather some form of light coverage is a wise precaution.

## *Chaenomeles* (Rosaceae)

The well-known and familiar 'Japonica', the ornamental quince, despite its decorative role, often bears fruit capable of being made into very acceptable quince jelly. Perfectly hardy, it does not require wall treatment, but because it responds so well to a sunny position this seems to have become almost a traditional way of growing the plant. Certainly the open, typically rose-shaped flowers are more easily appreciated in this situation, opening as they do in late winter and early spring. Most of the varieties grown are the result of crosses between *C. japonica*, introduced from Japan in 1869 by Messrs Maule of Bristol, and first named as *Cydonia maulei*, and *C. speciosa*, introduced from China by Sir Joseph Banks in 1796. Leading nurseries list up to 40 varieties, of which the following are some of the best.

| | |
|---|---|
| 'Cardinalis' | Crimson scarlet. |
| 'Moerloosii' | Pink and white. |
| 'Nivalis' | Large pure white. |
| 'Phylis Moore' | Semi-double, pink. |
| 'Simonii' | Semi-double, blood-red, suitable for low walls. |

'Boule de Feu'        Orange-red.
'Crimson and Gold'    Crimson with golden anthers.
'Knap Hill Scarlet'   Orange-scarlet.
'Rowallane'           Large blood crimson.

As wall plants they need to be trained to wires or supports and pruned rather like apple trees, the branches spurred back after flowering and in late summer the outward-pointing growths shortened back to 4 or 6 buds to encourage the formation of spurs. Some kind of framework should be maintained but old and worn out wood cut out. Propagated by cuttings of semi-ripe wood in June or by layering. Hardy in Zone 5 in the USA where it appears to be more often grown as a free-standing shrub, hedge plant or windbreak.


*Chimonanthus praecox* (**Calycanthaceae**) (**13**)

Wintersweet, the common name for this shrub, describes effectively its two great virtues; it flowers in the depth of winter, from December to February, and the flowers borne on bare twigs are heavily scented. It is perfectly hardy in the open but is more frequently grown as a wall plant; wall protection induces slightly earlier flowering and possibly provides easier inspection and enjoyment of the flowers. These are neither large nor colourful, about 1 in (2.5 cm) in length, and consist of an outer ring of pale yellow petals and an inner ring of dull purple. The pointed, light green leaves which appear in spring have a curiously rough upper surface, presumably a form of protection against browsing animals. It is certainly effective against slugs and snails.

On mature plants a few flowers will sometimes set giving rise to light green, flask-shaped fruits. When in the following year the seeds and soft matter disperse, the stalk and veins of the fruits persist hanging like miniature lanterns, of interest though of no special beauty. Not a plant for the impatient gardener since it seldom gives flower until it has been established for some years, rarely less than seven. It is best propagated by seed or layering, as cuttings are slow and not easy to root. The flowers, a few of which when cut will scent a room, are borne on shoots of the previous spring matured through the summer. Pruning is not necessary other than to keep the plant within bounds; it should be done not later than February and comprise the shortening back of over-long twigs and stems. Several clones showing slight variations are in existence, five are identified and described in *Curtis's Botanical Magazine* (New Series t.184), but apart from the variety 'Lutea', which has totally yellow flowers and reputedly less scent, these are not likely to be listed by nurserymen.

The generic name is derived from the Greek *cheimo* meaning 'winter' and *anthos* meaning 'flower'. Introduced from China in 1766 by Lord Coventry, it was first grown at his seat in Worcestshire. It was illustrated and delightfully described in *Curtis's Botanical Magazine* (t.466) in the year 1800 as *Calycanthus praecox*. It is still occasionally listed in catalogues as such, but more often as *Chimonanthus fragrans*, although botanically *Chimonanthus praecox* is correct. Whatever the name it is true that, as that great plantsman the late E. A. Bowles wrote, '*Chimonanthus* is indispensable and should be planted in any garden large enough to hold two plants.'

## *Choisya ternata* (Rutaceae)

The protection of a wall is not essential for this, the 'Mexican Orange Blossom', but the flower buds from which the white, lightly-scented flowers are produced are susceptible to searing March winds and early morning sun after frost; it is therefore a candidate for west-facing walls. Once established in reasonable soil it grows vigorously and will make a rounded bush some 5 ft (1.5 m) high by 6 ft (1.8 m) across, thus substantial border provision is necessary in front of the wall. Its rounded form of growth and bright green evergreen leaves make it a good shrub for a west-facing corner site. If its stature has to be restricted it may be pruned back after flowering. At that time young growth will break readily from older wood.

The specific name refers to the trifoliate leaves whose bright fresh green make an ideal foil for the umbels of white, five-petalled fragrant flowers profusely produced in April and May. The leaves when crushed have a strong pungent scent difficult to describe. The plant may be propagated by means of cuttings of

63

half-ripened wood taken in June–July and inserted in a sand frame in gentle heat. As the common name suggests it is a native of Mexico and was introduced as long ago as 1825, but by whom is not clear. The generic name, *Choisya*, honours a Swiss botanist, M. Jacques-Denis Choisy (1799–1859).

## *Clematis* (Ranunculaceae)

A genus with members that provide flower from January to October and which in beauty vie with the rose for the place of supreme flowering climber. They climb by twisting their leaf stalks around any suitable twig or stem and are at their best climbing up and through some supporting bush or tree; as wall plants, some form of wire or lattice for support is essential. They can be grown as individual features, particularly the large-flowered kinds, upon a tripod of poles (*see* Fig. 5) or single larch poles with short side branches retained. In this situation they can be combined with climbing roses to give a succession of colour. The Jackmanii types are best for this purpose since these grow

*Fig. 5  A tripod of poles used as a support for clematis.*

64

perfectly well if cut back in autumn, the climbing rose being pruned at the same time.

The word clematis generally conjures up visions of the large-petalled purple Jackmanii. Raised by Jackmans of Woking, Surrey, in 1860 this was presumed to be a cross between *C. lanuginosa* and *C. viticella* and remains a lasting memorial to a firm whose notable horticultural history was sadly terminated by the death in 1977 of Rowland Jackman. In addition to *C. jackmanii* there are a number of other species and varieties valued as climbers and they are here described in the order in which they flower in British gardens. In general they are perfectly hardy and can be recommended as Zone 4–5 plants in the USA. The cultivars are propagated by cuttings, layering or by grafting onto stocks of the wild *C. vitalba*; species may be grown from seed.

First, indeed flowering unobtrusively through the winter, is the all too seldom grown *C. cirrhosa* var. *balearica*. With finely divided, almost fern-like foliage it is a plant for a sheltered wall spot where its 1 to 2 in (2.5 to 5 cm) white-cream flowers can be savoured on mild winter days; an earlier name was *C. calycina* and it is sometimes catalogued as that.

In April the evergreen *C. armandii* shows its flowers; of rather straggling habit, it demands a fair portion of wall space, for which position it is most suitable. The variety 'Apple Blossom' should be sought; the white sepals are larger than those of the type and delicately flushed pink.

The spring-flowering *C. alpina* is a climber for low walls. The lovely nodding blue flowers have petal-like growths, staminodes, that give an impression of double flowers. A native of Eastern Asia it has been in gardens since 1792. The best clone is 'Frances Rivis'.

The month of May brings the full glory of *C. montana*. Widely planted and universally admired it covers itself with 2 to $2\frac{1}{2}$ in (5 to 6 cm) flowers of white or pink; 'Grandiflora' is a large white form admirable against red brick walls. Of the pink-coloured kinds 'Elizabeth' and 'Tetrarose' (41) are good, 'Rubens' (14) is later flowering and slightly fragrant. As a climber for walls or trees *C. montana* is superb; in either its white or pink form it provides a breathtaking picture when draped over a dark green yew or similar conifer. It was introduced from the Himalayas in 1831.

On the heels of *C. montana* or sometimes flowering at the same time comes *C. macropetala*, a climber for low walls or fences. Introduced by the plant collector William Purdom (1880–1921), it first flowered at the Coombe Wood nursery of Messrs Veitch in 1912. It is native of Kansu, China and Siberia. Like *C. alpina* it has a number of petaloid segments in the flower giving the appearance of doubling; 'Markham's Pink' is a rose-coloured form and 'Maidwell Hall' a particularly good blue selection.

Following quickly on *C. montana* and *C. macropetela* come the large flowered varieties derived from *C. florida, C. lanuginosa* and *C. patens*. Within this group, flowering in May and June and often on into August comes the well-known 'Nelly Moser'. In addition to this fine variety there are the following, all suitable for walls, pillars or tripods.

| | |
|---|---|
| 'Barbara Dibley' (**16**) | Violet with dark-carmine stripes along each petal. |
| 'Beauty of Worcester' | Blue-violet with white stamens. |
| 'Belle of Woking' | Pale mauve. |
| 'Blue Gem' | Sky-blue. |
| 'Duchess of Edinburgh' | Large double white, slightly scented. |
| 'Fairy Queen' | Pale pink with brighter central bars, very large. |
| 'Henryi' (**15**) | Cream-white with dark stamens, large, vigorous. |
| 'Lasurstern' | Deep lavender-blue, prominent white stamens. |
| 'Nelly Moser' (**19**) | Pale mauve-pink, large with carmine central bar, best on north wall. |
| 'The President' | Deep purple-blue, free-flowering. |
| 'Percy Picton' | Purple. |
| 'Vyvian Pennell' | Deep violet-blue, double, May to July, sometimes produces single lavender-blue flowers in autumn. |
| 'Lady Londesborough' | Pale mauve, dark stamens. |

Carrying on the clematis cavalcade come the Jackmanii selections, worthy offspring of that 1860 cross. The following include some of the best.

| | |
|---|---|
| 'Comtesse de Bouchaud' | Soft rose-pink, yellow stamens, vigorous and free flowering. |
| 'Gypsy Queen' | Violet-purple, broad rounded sepals. |
| 'Hagley Hybrid' | Shell-pink with chocolate-brown stamens, lovely with yellow *Potentilla* or *Phlomis* in front or with *Hedera* 'Buttercup' as a background. |
| 'Jackmanii Superba' | Violet-purple, large, vigorous and free-flowering. |
| 'Mrs Cholmondely' | Pale blue, large. |
| 'Madame Edouard André' | Rich crimson with yellow stamens, free-flowering. |
| 'Perle d'Azure' (17) | Light blue with broad sepals, free-flowering. |

From summer into autumn we have *C. texensis* and *C. viticella*. In both, the hybrids and varieties are more colourful than the species. Those from *C. texensis* share in its red flower colour and slight tenderness. It hails from Texas and came to Britain around 1868. Hybrids which contain its blood and are excellent plants include 'Duchess of Albany', flowers somewhat tubular, bright pink shading to lilac and 'Gravetye Beauty', flowers more bell-shaped and cherry-red in colour.

The comparatively small flowers of the viticella hybrids are produced in profusion from late July to October; a plant very suitable for pergolas and informal situations. If a laburnum arch has been constructed (*see* plate **32**) this clematis is well suited to climb up and through the branches to give a late summer display. The stems may be pruned back to 2 or 3 ft (60–90 cm) in winter and will not interfere with the laburnum growth or flower. The number of fine viticella hybrids and varieties include the following.

| | |
|---|---|
| 'Ascotiensis' | Azure-blue, July to September. |
| 'Ernest Markham' | Glowing petunia-red. |
| 'Huldine' | Pearly-white, best in full sun, July to October. |
| 'Lady Betty Balfour' | Deep velvety-purple, yellow stamens, vigorous, best in full sun, August to October. |

67

| 'Abundance' | Veined flowers of soft purple. |
| 'Alba Luxurians' | White tinted mauve. |
| 'Kermesina' | Crimson. |
| 'Minuet' | Erect slightly large flowers, white with a band of purple at each sepal tip. |
| 'Royal Velours' | Deep velvety-purple. |

Autumn we tend to associate with *C. orientalis* (**18**) and its near relative, *C. tangutica*, for the seed heads of both species comprise silky clusters of feathered seeds which are particularly lovely when covered with autumn dews. Both make tangled masses of shoots with finely-divided grey-green leaves and the flowers of both are yellow, pendulous and nodding, but the form of *C. orientalis* discovered in the Himalayas by the plant explorers Ludlow and Sherriff in 1947 and available from nurseries under their collector's number L & S 13342 has attracted attention by the thickness of its deep yellow sepals, and is termed the 'Orange-Peel Clematis'. The flowers of *C. tangutica* are more delicate, lighter and clear yellow; excellent for low walls, it was introduced from Mongolia in about 1890.

Also flowering into October is *C. rehderana*; once known as *C. nutans*, it is a delightful species to train into a derelict tree. The small, primrose-yellow flowers are scented of cowslips. A gentle, pleasant plant introduced from Western China in 1898.

For the larger garden or for the wild garden, *C. vitalba*, our own native 'Traveller's Joy', should not be overlooked. A familiar climber over hedges and roadside trees in chalk or lime-stone areas. Few sights are more lovely and more evocative of winter than the hanging curtains of feathered seed heads covered with hoar frost. It is equally lovely in a quiet way in late summer when covered with masses of small, green-white, faintly-scented flowers. Too vigorous for small gardens but excellent in the wild garden or to cover dead or moribund trees.

Much is written on the pruning of *Clematis*, but in reality it is fairly simple. Taking them in flowering order, *C. cirrhosa* and *C. armandii* require no pruning other than the removal of dead wood. For *Clematis montana* on trees no pruning is needed or possible, but on walls or fences its very vigour may dictate occasional cutting back which should be done immediately after flowering. The large-flowered 'Nelly Moser' types need little pruning; cut out dead wood and shorten over-long vines to a pair of strong buds in February. The Jackmanii types should have all growth cut hard back to about 3 ft (1 m) above ground level in February or March. Similar treatment suits the late-flowering kinds, *C. viticella*, *C. orientalis* and *C. tangutica*, unless of course they are hosted by trees.

If this brief description of some of the best clematis has whetted the appetite, there are many more books on the subject, from *The Clematis as a Garden Flower* (Moore & Jackman 1877) to Christopher Lloyd's *Clematis* (1989) and Jim Fisk's *Clematis: The Queen of Climbers* (1989).

## *Clerodendrum* (Verbenaceae)

One species of *Clerodendrum* qualifies as a wall plant — *C. bungei*, more often known as *C. foetidum*. It is killed to the ground in most British winters but during the summer sends up erect shoots some 4 to 5 ft (1.2–1.5 m) high, bearing in August and September terminal heads of purple-red blossom. The small, crowded flowers are slightly fragrant but the leaves like those of other *Clerodendrums* have a nauseous smell when crushed.

A native of China, it was introduced by Robert Fortune in 1844, and is a useful wall plant because of its late-flowering season. Probably a Zone 7 plant in the USA with the rootstock needing winter cover. It is readily propagated by suckers.

## *Clianthus* (Leguminosae) (20)

The flower of *Clianthus puniceus* is the most exotic of any climber or wall plant hardy in Britain. The only species of the genus worth trying out of doors, it is a 'risk' plant even in the southern counties of Britain and in any Zone below 9 in the USA. Since it is a plant that is readily and cheaply propagated from seed it is a risk that could be taken more often.

In suitable conditions it will achieve a height of 10 ft (3 m) and is evergreen with pinnate, light-green leaves. The generic name is from the Greek meaning 'glory flower', and the flowers certainly live up to that description. They are produced in early summer, with pendulous stems carrying at their ends clusters of the curious brilliant red flowers. These are basically structured like a pea flower but with elongated standards and curved keels that justify the common names of 'Parrot's Bill' and 'Lobster Claw'. A native of New Zealand, it was introduced to Britain in 1831.

Specimens in the southern counties of Britain have survived quite severe winters when planted in light, well-drained soil and set against a south wall. There is a white-flowered form but to my mind this is of interest only to the specialist plantsman.

## Cobaea (Polemoniaceae) (21)

The 'Cup and Saucer' plant or 'Cathedral Bells', *C. scandens*, is a perennial climber that only too often in Britain has to be treated as an annual. Happily it is easily raised under glass from seed, and if planted out sufficiently early will flower from August to October. If the roots can be adequately protected, and this is possible in mild areas, it can be treated as a perennial and will flower slightly earlier. Growth is rapid and extensive and it is often necessary to steer the stem back towards ground level lest the flowers are borne so high up as to be of no interest. It is a good plant for pergolas where the growth can be trained horizontally but the situation must be protected, sunny and south-facing.

*Cobaea scandens* was introduced as long ago as 1787 from Central America. It climbs by means of tendrils at the ends of the pinnate leaves which have ovate to elliptical leaflets. The flower, carried on an 8 in (20 cm) stalk, opens as a pale greenish-purple trumpet (the 'cup'), which is about 2 in (5 cm) long, becoming darker purple as it develops and sitting on a calyx of five green sepals which fold back to give the 'saucer' effect. The plant came to Britain via Spain and was first recorded here in 1784 when it was figured beautifully and accurately in *Curtis's Botanical Magazine* (t.851). From this we learn that it was named in honour of the Jesuit Father Cobo (1572–1659), a Spanish missionary who resided for more than 40 years in Central America. There is a white form 'Flore Albo' and one with variegated leaves that has to be perpetuated by propagation by cuttings.

## *Colquhounia* (Labiatae)

The generic name, not the easiest, was bestowed by the botanist Dr Wallich (1786–1854) to compliment his friend Sir Robert Colquhoun, a patron of the Calcutta Botanic Garden of which Wallich was Director. The predominant species, *C. coccinea* from Nepal, was described by Dr Wallich in 1822 and figured in *Curtis's Botanical Magazine* in 1850 (t.4514) from material grown at Kew. A slightly different form raised from seed sent home by the plant collector F. Kingdon Ward (1885–1958) was pictured in the same magazine (New Series t.115) in 1950, exactly 100 years later. The shrub described from Kew in 1850 had dull green, rather soft, ovate-lanceolate leaves and whorls of scarlet and orange-red, slightly striped, labiate flowers like a very large and very colourful dead-nettle. Plants growing against the wall of the temperate house at Kew today appear exactly the same.

In Britain the shrub flowers at the summer's end and its display is very dependent on prevailing weather. The plant's variability is shown by two forms in circulation at the present time, *C.* var. *mollis* with leaves bearing additional indumentum and *C.* var. *vestita*, said to be hardier than the type. *Colquhounia* is a wall plant of character and interest which can be cut to the ground by sharp frosts, although it will grow again from the base and can attain some 5 or 6 ft (1.5–1.8 m). Propagated by cuttings of summer shoots set in sand in gentle heat. Doubtless a Zone 8 plant in the USA.

## *Cotoneaster* (Rosaceae)

A number of the small-leaved *Cotoneasters* have a trailing habit, but some of these such as *C. microphylla* and *C. congestus* although sometimes planted against walls are better suited as rock garden plants.

For walls the *Cotoneaster* of proven value is *C. horizontalis*, whose interesting 'fishbone' arrangement of stems seems designed by nature to lay flat against wall surfaces. The plant is deciduous, the small $\frac{1}{2}$ in (1.3 cm) dark-green leaves complementing the scarlet berries strung like beads along the

71

stems. The small pink flowers that precede them are attractive, particularly so to bees. A native of China it was introduced by the Jesuit missionary Père David (1826–1900) who sent seeds to Paris around 1870. There is a variegated leaved form which unfortunately is very shy to flower and berry (22).

The plant will naturally hug the wall but the main stems should be tied in lest snow and wind break them away. Completely hardy in Britain and to Zone 5 in the USA, it is an excellent plant for north or east walls and will accept a wide range of soils. Pruning is only necessary to remove old worn-out portions. Propagated easily by seed or cuttings of semi-ripe wood.

## Crinodendron (Elaeocarpaceae)

A genus having two species that in most of Britain must be treated as wall plants. The best known, C. hookerianum, is somewhat stiff in habit with dark-green, lanceolate leaves and pendulous coral-red flowers that look like closed lanterns. An evergreen attaining 30 ft (9 m) in favourable circumstances but more usually about 12 ft (3.5 m), it needs a cool, moist peaty soil and the protection of a west-facing wall. A native of Chile, introduced by William Lobb (1809–1865) when collecting for the nurserymen Messrs Veitch in 1848, it is still sometimes called by the earlier name of Tricuspidaria lanceolata.

The second species, C. patagua, also a native of Chile, was introduced by H. J. Elwes (1846–1922), the celebrated arboriculturist, in 1901. It is very unlike C. hookerianum, as the evergreen leaves are oval, and the flowers are white, bell-shaped and pendulous with five petals that have indentations at the apex giving the flowers a 'fringed' appearance. A rapid grower, it appears to be more hardy than C. hookerianum. Both are easily increased by cuttings and both need and merit Zone 9 treatment in the USA, combined of course with suitable soil and moisture. Prune only to remove dead wood.

## Cytisus battandieri (Leguminosae) (23)

A 'broom' that is totally unlike the usual conception of broom; a broom bearing a wealth of yellow, flower-clustered trusses each like a large bottle brush and with a delightful fruity scent, justifying its popular name of 'Pineapple Broom'. Suprisingly, although hailing from North Africa, an area botanised over many years, it was not found until 1915 when M. P. E. de Peyerimhoff discovered it at 5000 to 6000 ft (1500 to 1800 m) in the Atlas mountains of Morocco. The specific name honours the botanist Prof. Jules Aimé Battandier (1848–1922).

It is reasonably hardy in Britain, indeed Bean (*Trees and Shrubs Hardy in the British Isles*) records that it came through the harsh winter of 1962–3. He draws attention also to the beautiful leaves covered with satiny down; each comprises three leaflets, the silvery grey-green making a lovely foil for the lemon-yellow flowers. Grown as a wall plant and strategically tied in, its rather lax habit has protection from winds which otherwise can blow it over. Pruning is generally unnecessary, but old wood should occasionally be removed allowing its replacement by young growths from the base. As might be expected a light dry soil suits it best; in the USA it is a Zone 5 shrub.

Introduced to Britain in 1922 it was illustrated in *Curtis's Botanical Magazine* (New Series t.10–1948) where attention is drawn to the variance in flowering among different clones. With this in mind and the fact that propagation is by seed or budding on seedling laburnum, it is wise when purchasing to ask for budded plants since these are more likely to have come from one of the better flowered clones.

## *Decumaria* (Hydrangeaceae)

A genus of two species both needing sheltered east or west walls but in nature ascending tree trunks by means of aerial rootlets like ivy. The deciduous *D. barbara*, which can reach 30 ft (9 m), has opposite, oval to ovate leaves glabrous on both sides. The flowers, individually small, $\frac{1}{4}$in (5 mm) across, are borne on erect terminal corymbs 3 in (7.5 cm) long in late June and July. It is a native of the eastern United States. The other species, *D. sinensis*, is evergreen and rarely exceeds 15 ft (4.5 m). The leaves are rounded, and the flowers yellowish-white and fragrant. A native of Central China, it was introduced in 1908. Zone 7 in the USA, plants may be propagated by cuttings made in August from semi-ripe wood inserted in sand/peat in a close frame. The

73

CLIMBERS AND WALL PLANTS

generic name is derived from the Latin *decimus* and refers to the numbers of the flower parts, petals 7 to 10, and stamens 20 to 30.

## *Dendromecon* (Papaveraceae)

There are records of some fine specimens of this wall shrub in Britain, but always sooner or later they appear to have succumbed to one of our more severe winters; for gambling gardeners this is the shrub *par excellence*.

The Yellow Tree Poppy, *D. rigida*, is a lovely plant. The ovate, slightly thick, 2 to 3 in (5–8 cm) long leaves, grey-green and glaucous, the flowers like bright yellow poppies 2 in (5 cm) in diameter with a central boss of stamens and slightly fragrant are produced intermittently through the summer. The plant should be tied in and trained to the wall at the onset of autumn so as to benefit from any residual warmth coming from the bricks. This training also assists in the better display of the following year's flowers. An open light soil suits it with the addition of some mortar rubble and of course a sunny south wall.

Propagated by shoots of ripened summer wood in sandy compost in heat. It is a native of California, a Zone 9 plant, and was first introduced to Britain by William Lobb in 1854. The generic name is from the Greek *Dendron*, 'a tree' and *mecon*, 'a poppy'.

## *Desfontainea* (Potaliaceae)

One of the most unusual-looking wall plants that can be grown in Britain, *Desfontainea spinosa* looks to the casual eye like a holly bush festooned with red and yellow flowers, almost an artificial decoration. Closer examination of the flowers which are borne in late summer shows them to be funnel-shaped, about $1\frac{1}{2}$ in (4 cm) long by $\frac{1}{2}$ in (1.3 cm) wide and scarlet with five yellow lobes. They are well set off by the glossy, dark green, prickle-edged leaves. A native of the Andes it was introduced by William Lobb (1809–1863) from Chile in 1843 and again by a modern collector, Harold Comber (1897–1969), in 1925. It grows well on the west coast of Scotland and in Northern Ireland, a moist, frost-free climate suiting it best. An interesting wall shrub well worth trying in a sheltered west-facing corner, probably a Zone 8 plant in the USA. Propagated by cuttings of semi-ripe wood which require to be under mist in a fairly warm house and are not easy to root.

## *Eccremocarpus* (Bignoniaceae)

South America has given us many fine shrubs that are on the border-line of hardiness in Britain and often require wall protection to give of their best; *Eccremocarpus scaber* the only species of the genus in general cultivation is one of these. Introduced from Chile as long ago as 1824, it is a semi-woody climber of doubtful hardiness except in the south, but so quick-growing as to be treated as an annual. For this purpose seed should be sown in February in heat and the potted young plants put out in May. Given mild winters it will persist and make a woody base.

Growth is straggling and leafage sparse, the leaves ending in a tendril which will grasp any suitable support, against a wall it requires pea sticks or wire mesh. The orange-red flowers produced continuously from June onwards are in racemes of 6 to 12, and the plant sets seed readily. The lower stems are usually rather bare so visually it benefits by having a low bushy plant before it; alternatively it can be so planted as to climb towards and up a supporting plant such as *Azara, Chaenomeles* or *Jasminum nudiflorum*. There is a clear yellow variety 'Aureus' which makes a charming picture climbing up and through blue *Caryopteris*, itself a useful wall shrub.

## *Euonymus* (Celastraceae)

One species from this large genus of mostly free-standing berrying shrubs has proved a most useful and versatile ground and wall climbing plant. This is *E. fortunei* var. *radicans* a creeping evergreen Japanese shrub whose manner of growth is similar to that of ivy (*see Hedera*, page 83). It will climb trees or walls by means of adhering rootlets like ivy, sometimes to the height of 20 ft (6 m) and when ceasing to creep or climb will produce larger leaves and bear flowers and fruit. In this respect it is very different from other members of its genus. It is very

75

hardy (Zone 4) and used in America on house walls in place of ivy in areas where ivy is not hardy. In Britain it is extremely useful for coverage on north or east walls.

Nurserymen list several colour forms all of which are easily propagated by planting rooted portions or inserting stem cuttings in a sand frame. The usual green-leaved variety is *E. var. radicans*, often called in the trade *Euonymus radicans* or just 'Radicans'; the leaves are ovate-elliptic up to $1\frac{1}{2}$ in (3.5 cm) long, shallow-toothed and leathery in texture. 'Variegatus' is the white variegated form, very attractive; it was introduced from Japan in 1860. 'Coloratus' has $2\frac{1}{2}$ in (6 cm) leaves which are coloured red-purple throughout winter and will often resume green coloration in spring. Finally there is 'Kewensis', a minute form with leaves $\frac{1}{4}$ to $\frac{5}{8}$ in (6–8 mm) introduced to Kew from Japan in 1893, only suited needless to say to very low walls.

## Fatsia japonica (Araliaceae)

A familiar sight in seaside gardens, the large palmate and divided leaves of *Fatsia* have a semi-tropical appearance. Indeed it was often used as a 'fixed piece' in the 'tropical' bedding that was beloved in Edwardian England, and is returning to popularity in some of our public parks today. Although it flourishes in the tolerant climate of south-coast seaside towns it is, given wall protection and a slightly shady situation, hardy in most of Britain. It is a doubtful Zone 7 in the USA.

The plant can make an impressive bush some 6 to 8 ft (1.5 to 2.5 m) high, bearing large umbels of creamy-white flowers very similar to the flowers of ivy, to which plant it is related (indeed *Fatshedera*, that popular houseplant, is a cross between *Fatsia* and *Hedera helix* 'Hibernica'). A native of Japan and grown in Britain since 1838, it is not particular as to soil and requires no pruning unless its 12 to 16 in (30 to 40 cm) leaves overwhelm some choicer subject.

## Feijoa (Myrtaceae)

An interesting and unusual wall shrub with the added attraction of edible flower petals! *Feijoa sellowiana* was discovered in Brazil

76

in 1819 by a German plant collector named Sellow. The generic name honours Don Feijo, a Spanish botanist. Like so many South American shrubs it is only a possibility for the warmer parts of Britain and not below Zone 8 in the USA.

The plant forms in Britain a rounded bush or small tree rarely more than some 6 by 8 ft (1.8 to 2.4 m); if it flourishes it will need at least 6 ft (1.8 m) of border in front of the south-facing wall against which it should be placed. The neat grey-green leaves with almost white undersides make a good backing for the attractive flowers. These are about 2 in (5 cm) long and have comparatively thick greyish-white petals around a prominent cluster of long red stamens tipped with yellow anthers. Reference was earlier made to the edibility of the petals — they are indeed pleasantly sweet, slightly thick and juicy and worth trying on thin bread and butter! I have not seen fruit produced in this country but it too is edible as one might expect from the plant's relationship to the *Guava*. Although reputed to be somewhat capricious in flowering, it is a plant worth trying in a sheltered spot. It does well at Kew and may do best on light dry soils which encourage summer ripening of the wood. Propagated by cuttings of half-ripened wood in heat; no pruning is needed.

## *Fendlera* (Philadelphaceae)

The only species of *Fendlera* in cultivation has been described as a beautiful but difficult plant to grow and this is a very fair summary. The species is *F. rupicola* var. *wrightii* which makes a deciduous shrub to about 6 ft (1.8 m) high with small $\frac{1}{2}$ to $1\frac{1}{2}$ in (1–4 cm) long, lanceolate, roughly hairy leaves. The white or pink-tinted flowers borne in May are four-petalled, each petal constricted towards its base making an open, very elegant flower.

A native of the south-western United States down to northern Mexico, it was introduced into Europe around 1879. It comes from sun-drenched mountain slopes and is only successful in the driest, sunniest parts of eastern England and with the protection of a south-facing wall. In such a situation it is well worth trying. Propagated by cuttings of soft summer wood set in sand in gentle heat. USA Zone 8–9, in dry areas.

## *Ficus* (Moraceae)

Figs have been traditional wall plants for hundreds of years in Britain, but not being considered as ornamentals are outside the scope of this book. One member of the genus that is an ornamental, however, and can be grown outside in parts of Britain, is *F. pumila* or *F. repens*, as it is sometimes called.

It is a neat evergreen climber whose leaves, close set in opposite rows are about $\frac{3}{4}$ to $1\frac{1}{4}$ in (2–3 cm) long and half as wide. The leaves change character when the plant reaches some 10 or 12 ft (3–3.5 m) becoming much larger, then if conditions are suitable, flowers and fruit develop. In this respect it is not unlike ivy (*Hedera*). A native of China and Japan, it is known to have been in cultivation here in the mid-eighteenth century usually as a conservatory or cool greenhouse plant. The existence out of doors in Sussex and Cornwall of some quite large and old specimens suggests that it could be more widely planted in the milder areas of Britain. In the USA it is valued as a climber in California and the south (Zones 8–9).

## *Forsythia* (Oleaceae)

This extensively-planted shrub whose bright yellow flowers wreathe its bare stems in March is better known under its botanical name than the rather fanciful and artificial one of 'Golden Bells'. The name honours William Forsythe (1737–1804), gardener to King George III at Kensington and St James's, a Scot and one of the founders of the Royal Horticultural Society. Forsythe in his superintendence of the Kensington gardens turned his mind to the healing of tree wounds necessitated by the removal of large branches of the rather decrepit fruit trees that he found when taking over the garden. He devised a 'plaister', a combination of cow dung, lime, wood ashes, sand, soap suds and urine, calling it his 'composition' and drawing attention to its advantages in healing tree wounds. England was at war with Napoleon and sound oak for ships was at a premium. In 1789 a Parliamentary Commission, convinced that Forsythe's composition would benefit the oak trees of the nation, recommended to the King a

78

reward, reported to have been £1500, for the secrets of the 'composition'. The composition was of course eventually shown to be useless.

With one exception, the rare *F. europaea*, the *Forsythias* are natives of Eastern Asia, and were introduced into Britain between 1845 and 1857. In addition to *F. europaea* four species are known and one group of hybrids. Strangely there is no record of a white form or a double. As wall plants the following are the most suitable. *F. x intermedia* 'Spectabilis' **(24)**, one of the hybrids, is probably the most widely planted of all, producing masses of closely-packed golden flowers. It was raised by Späth of Berlin around 1906. *F. x intermedia* 'Lynwood' is a bud sport of 'Spectabilis', introduced in 1935, equally floriferous but it differs in having a shorter but broader petal. A little later in flowering and with paler flowers, *F. suspensa* 'Atrocaulis' has stems of a distinctive brown purple, a good choice against a white wall; unfortunately it is seldom offered by nurseries. *F. suspensa* itself straggles outwards too much for any but the largest of walls.

*Forsythia x intermedia* 'Beatrix Farrand' is one of a group of colchicine-induced tetraploids raised at the Arnold Arboretum in America around 1944. Plant mutations in which the chromosome numbers are enhanced or altered occur occasionally in nature, and the drug colchicine has been successfully used to induce mutations which sometimes result in plants larger in leaf or flower. 'Beatrix Farrand' has individual flowers double the size of others but as one might expect they are more sparingly produced, although more elegant and excellent for cutting.

*Forsythias* are really shrubs for the open border, and wall protection is unnecessary in Britain or the USA where it is a Zone 5 plant. If, however, an area of north or east wall has to be covered they can prove very decorative and colourful. The plant will need to be tied in to the wall; pruning out branches after they have flowered and tying in the young strong growths will result in the plant regularly covering itself each March with sheets of golden flowers.

## *Fremontodendron* (Sterculiaceae)

One of the number of good plants that have come to us from California. The most commonly grown species, *Fremontodendron*

79

*californica*, was discovered by Capt. J. C. Frémont in 1846 during his exploration of Western America, and the genus bears his name. The plant was introduced to Britain shortly afterwards and first flowered in the Chiswick garden of the Horticultural Society in 1854.

Forming a shrub or small tree it is partially evergreen, the dull green of the leaves enlivened by the pale brown hairs that cover the under-surface. The single 2 in (5 cm) golden yellow flowers are held mostly at right angles to the stem tending to face the onlooker and make a fine display from May to July. What appear to be the five petals of the flower are in fact the five lobes of the calyx; petals as such are absent. A hybrid between *F. californica* and the similar but more tender species *F. mexicana* was raised in 1952 and named 'California Glory' (**25**). The name is justified, as with its larger flowers and greater vigour it is better than either parent. Whereas the parent species are readily raised from seed, 'California Glory' being a hybrid has to be propagated by cuttings which do not root easily. Many nurseries, however, have mastered the technique, and the plant is now readily available. In Britain *Fremontodendrons* succeed only in the warmer areas and even there require wall protection. They are best on fairly light, well-drained poorish soils; winter wet can be their undoing. Pruning is not necessary but plants should be carefully tied in to the wall.

## *Fuchsia* (Onagraceae)

According to tradition the fuchsia was introduced to Britain by James Lee (1715–1795), an eminent Hammersmith nurseryman who obtained his plant from a sailor's wife in Wapping. Another story has it that a certain Captain Firth in 1788 brought an apparently dead plant from Lisbon to Kew where it sprouted and grew. Both stories may be true, as the plant is a native of Brazil and seafarers at that time were responsible for many intro-ductions. The plant so introduced has been identified as *F. coccinea*, and with *F. magellanica*, a Chilean species, introduced around 1820, was the parent of many of our present-day varieties.

A number are good wall plants particularly where the border in front of the wall is narrow, even the taller kinds if planted fairly close to the wall will take up little more than 2 or 3 ft (60–90 cm) and in such a situation will survive in most parts of Britain although they may be cut to the ground in severe weather. The hardiest of the taller kinds is *F. magellanica* 'Riccartonii'. Raised at Riccarton in Scotland in 1830 it has typical fuschia-shaped flowers, the scarlet sepals surrounding a small 'skirt' of violet petals and long extruding stamens. In mild areas it makes hedges and bushes of considerable size. Widely grown and deservedly so is *F. magellanica* 'Versicolor', with grey-green leaves, rose-tinted and irregularly variegated creamy-white, a lovely backing for its scarlet flowers.

The delicately-flowered 'Madame Cornelissen' with rose-scarlet calyx and white petals is quite hardy, as is the rather taller soft pink 'Chillerton Beauty'. Shorter and more bushy varieties are 'Alice Hoffman', scarlet calyx and white petals, 'Elsa', striking with white calyx and double violet and rose petals, and an old favourite, 'Mrs Popple', scarlet calyx and violet petals. These are shrubs of almost bedding habit but very suitable as wall plants in very narrow borders.

Fuchsias are easily propagated by soft-wood cuttings taken in late summer and rooted in sandy compost without heat, the young plants being wintered in frost free conditions. A Zone 7 plant in the USA, the generic name honours Leonard Fuchs (1501–1566), a German botanist.

## *Garrya elliptica* (Garryaceae) (26)

Any plant that flowers in January or February is sure of a welcome in gardens in the Northern hemisphere and the profusely produced catkins of this excellent shrub reliably cheer winter's days. *Garrya* is dioecious, in other words individual plants bear flowers of one sex only; the male flowers, the pollen producers, borne on long catkins, are more striking than the shorter catkins of the seldom grown female form.

Although *Garrya* is not a climber it makes a very good wall plant albeit requiring a fair amount of room. It should not be placed in an unduly prominent position since it has one drawback in that the dead flowers, the dessicated catkins, hang

81

over-long on the plant, often to mid-summer and past before they are obliterated by new growth. Although a west-facing wall or corner suits it best, it will do quite well on north or east walls provided that they are sheltered from extreme wind.

The evergreen ovate leaves are 2 to 3 in (5 to 7 cm) long and about half as wide; dark grey-green above they are grey beneath, an unusual feature being the curly hairs of the underside. The yellow-powdered catkins are from 3 to 6 in (7 to 15 cm) long but up to 12 in (30 cm) in warm favoured districts. It does not require a rich soil, flowering best on a slightly dry and poor soil. Planted against a wall it will attain 12 to 15 ft (3.5 to 4.5 m). It can be wall-trained but this is a constant task and it is best to allow some 4 to 6 ft (1.2 to 1.8 m) of border in front of its wall position for 'middle age spread'. Pruning can only comprise cutting back if the plant encroaches overmuch and this should be done in March or April. It is a plant that does not move well, and must be pot or container grown. Cuttings taken in late summer and kept in gentle heat root readily.

The plant was introduced by the explorer David Douglas who sent it home from California in 1828. It first bloomed in the Horticultural Society's garden at Chiswick in 1834. The name honours Nicholas Garry, Deputy Governor of the Hudson Bay Company from 1822 to 1835, after whom Fort Garry and Lake Garry are also named. The help of the Hudson Bay Company made Douglas' journeys possible; he used their ships, lodges, guides and interpreters and appeared to be on very good terms with Garry. The pendent catkin flowers have a classic simplicity, and W. J. Bean and others have noted the resemblance to the designs of Robert Adam's architectural festoons and swages, but it is doubtful if *Garrya* was the inspiration, for Adam had died before the plant had been seen in Britain.

A recently-introduced variation of the species is *Garrya elliptica* 'James Roof'. This occurred in a batch of seedlings raised at the Regional Parks Botanic Garden near Berkeley, California. A vigorous male form selected for the length of its catkins, up to 14 in (35 cm), Bean records that it was named in honour of the Garden Director. It is available from a few nurseries and is worth seeking by anyone intending to plant a *Garrya*.

## *Grevillea* (Proteaceae)

An Australian genus, some species of which can be grown as wall plants in climatically-favoured parts of Britain. The name honours Charles Francis Greville (1749–1809), second son of the Ist Earl of Warwick, Member of Parliament and friend of George III. Greville, despite his wealth, lived modestly and involved himself deeply in botany and horticulture. He was one of the seven founders of the Royal Horticultural Society and one of its first Vice-Presidents.

The flowers of the *Grevilleas* are curious and interesting. There is no calyx or corolla as such but a perianth cup which splits or sometimes opens into four as the flower develops, so releasing the long curved style that rises out of the incurved perianth, portions giving the flower its characteristic 'spiky' appearance.

Two species are well worth planting against south-facing walls in mild areas. One, *G. rosmarinifolia*, bears in June shrimp-red flowers on loose, graceful branches set with stalkless greyish evergreen leaves very similar to rosemary. The other, *G. sulphurea*, makes an evergreen bush of more sturdy habit not unlike a conifer in appearance, bearing in May among its rich green needles pale yellow flowers with the typically long curved styles.

*Grevilleas* may be propagated by half-ripened shoots taken in July and inserted in a peat/sand frame with bottom heat. Probably Zone 8 plants in the USA, they benefit from a dressing of peat, dislike lime or chalk and require a well-drained soil.

## *Hedera* (Araliaceae)

Acclaimed as the finest evergreen climber for temperate climes, the ivy, a widespread European and Asiatic plant, has a long history. It featured in the worship of Bacchus, the god of drink and festivity, and in the triumphal garlands of the Roman soldiers, and Pliny in his *Natural History* described three kinds, one of which was variegated. In medieval times a 'bush' of its adult-flowering stage was the sign of an alehouse, hence the phrase 'good wine needs no bush'.

Ivy adheres to buildings and trees by small rootlets, which are not parasitic and will not damage walls or masonry that is in good order. It is fair to point out, however, that when ivy gets to the top of its support the leaf shape changes and the plant throws out flowering shoots. If this bunchy adult growth receives an accumulation of snow it becomes top-heavy, and if the wall is in poor condition the extra weight may pull the top off. Ivy has many uses, and some varieties are popular as houseplants; but here we are concerned with it as wall, building or shed coverage, and for these purposes the following are some of the best available.

### *H. canariensis* 'Gloire de Marengo'

A native of North Africa and the Canary Islands; in this variety the young growth has bright cream-yellow variegation changing with age to a pleasant silvery variegation of the 3 to 4 in (7–10 cm) leaves. The least hardy of all ivies, it is prone to wind and frost scorch in winter. On wind-sheltered walls and away from early morning sun it makes quick-growing wall covering and a pleasant background for bright flowering plants.

### *H. colchica*

The Persian or 'Elephant's Ear' ivy, introduced from the Caucasus around 1851, is perfectly hardy, its large, unlobed 9 × 3 in (22 × 8 cm) leaves hanging like overlapping tiles. The variegated form of it, 'Dentata Variegata', introduced by L. R. Russell Ltd of Windlesham, Surrey, in 1908, has been called the best variegated evergreen climber in existence. The leaves are liberally splashed with cream-yellow variegation and like its green counterpart it is completely hardy. A more recent introduction is 'Sulphur Heart' (27), sometimes called 'Paddy's Pride', which has a slightly longer, narrower leaf and a lighter more central spread of yellow variegation.

### *H. helix*

This, the native ivy of Great Britain, is capable of a wide range of leaf variation. These variants with their different leaf shapes and colours are more attractive than common ivy and make excellent climbers.

'ANGULARIS AUREA' A good ivy for high walls; in young plants the leaves are slightly suffused with yellow, on mature plants in adult growth whole trusses of leaves turn bright yellow and appear against the normal green growth like yellow flowers.

'ATROPURPUREA' One of several ivies whose leaves turn purple in winter, an attribute that can be put to good effect by using them as backgrounds to early-flowering shrubs such as *Forsythia*. Others for this purpose are 'Woeneri' and 'Glymii' which has very glossy leaves.

'BUTTERCUP' An ivy to be grown in a good light situation when the leaves will take on the characteristic butter-yellow colour making it a remarkably attractive plant in its own right and a splendid background for purple clematis or blue *Caryopteris*.

'CAVENDISHII' One of the brightest ivies with what one might term white variegation and probably one of the oldest variegated plants known.

'DELTOIDEA' A dark green ivy with leaves varying from shield to heart-shaped. A favourite of that grand gardener the late E. A. Bowles and often called 'Bowles Shield Ivy'.

'GLACIER' A variegated ivy of soft, silvery-grey shades, very suitable to grow up and through a berrying shrub such as *Cotoneaster horizontalis*. Suited for low walls.

'GOLDHEART' Introduced from Italy in the 1950s this in its younger stages is the brightest and loveliest of all hardy ivies. The typically ivy-shaped dark green leaves each have a prominent central golden yellow 'splash'. This regular and intense variegation persists whilst the plant is climbing, but once it has reached the top of its support it has a tendency to throw green shoots and in time these being more vigorous can take over. Care in cutting out green shoots as they appear is well repaid.

'HIBERNICA' This, the so-called 'Irish Ivy', is a vigorous form with large slightly fluted leaves. In cultivation since early in the nineteenth century, it is extensively used as coverage for buildings including in Britain some notable and delightful inns. As with other ivies on buildings it should be clipped in March to remove old leaves and debris; at that time of year new growth and coverage will be rapid.

85

'PARSLEY CRESTED' This has light green leaves with heavily crimped edges. It is attractive and interesting, good for low walls, and the leaf crimp is more pronounced in plants in dry situations.

'PEDATA' The 'Bird's Foot Ivy' has a five-lobed leaf, the centre lobe long, the two lateral lobes at right angles and the two basal lobes back-pointing so as to give the effect of a bird's foot. A good and pleasant wall ivy.

'SAGITTIFOLIA VARIEGATA' This may be considered as a brightly variegated 'Bird's Foot Ivy', suitable for low walls, but can be frost or wind damaged.

'SULPHUREA' This has grey-green leaves overlaid with light sulphur-yellow, making it a fine background climber for brightly-coloured plants.

### H. nepalensis
The Nepal Ivy, introduced in the nineteenth century from the Himalayas, has russet-red stems and fairly long, 3 to 4 in (6 to 10 cm) narrow olive-green leaves with curiously 'stepped' margins. It is hardy but the young shoots are sometimes cut back by spring frosts. It grows well and is an interesting alternative to the common ivy.

Ivies will grow almost anywhere, although they prefer a soil with a fair lime content. They are easily propagated by summer or autumn cuttings or indeed by portions of young rooted runners. Apart from *H. canariensis* (Zone 7) they are Zone 5 plants in the USA where considerable attention is being paid to the plant and where trials to determine the hardiest varieties are in progress.

## Hoheria (Malvaceae)

Two species are of interest as wall plants. One is the deciduous *H. lyallii*, formerly called *Plagianthus lyallii*, and may still be seen in some catalogues under the latter name. It bears soft, bright green leaves, very downy on both surfaces, and in July clusters of white flowers, 1 to $1\frac{1}{2}$ in (2.5–4 cm) diameter, each with a central boss of purple stamens. A native of New Zealand and grown in Britain for a 100 years, it is reasonably hardy but is better given wall shelter.

The other species, *H. sexstylosa* (28), also from New Zealand, is evergreen, and although reasonably hardy in the south of Britain needs the shelter of a wall. The glossy, toothed, light green leaves, handsome at all times, are a background to its August display of clusters of white $\frac{3}{4}$ in (2 cm) flowers which have slightly pink styles. It is very floriferous and a most attractive shrub. A continental climate suits the *Hoherias* and one would assume them to be USA Zone 6 plants.

## *Holboellia* (Lardizabalaceae)

Evergreen twining climbers. *H. coriacea*, the hardiest of the two species grown, makes a vigorous plant up to 20 ft (6 m) with dark green, glossy, leathery leaves each comprising three stalked leaflets. The plant is monoecious, i.e. the flowers are either male or female but are borne separately on the same plant. The purplish male flowers each about $\frac{1}{2}$ in (1.2 cm) long are held in clusters at the ends of the shoots; the greenish-white, slightly larger female flowers form in axillary clusters lower down the plant. The slightly fragrant flowers appear in April and May and are very occasionally followed by fleshy, purple-coloured pod-like fruits. A native of China introduced by E. H. Wilson (1876–1930) in 1907 it is a hardy and useful, although not showy, climber over a small tree or on walls, a Zone 7 plant in the USA.

The other species, *H. latifolia*, introduced from the Himalayas in 1840, is less hardy but deliciously fragrant, otherwise similar in all respects to *H. coriacea*. Its lack of hardiness makes it a Zone 8 plant in the USA. Both species may be propagated by seed or by cuttings of semi-ripe wood in sand in a warm frame.

## *Humulus* (Cannabidaceae)

The hop, *Humulus lupulus*, is a native plant to Britain whose flower heads with their active ingredient lupulin (hence the specific name) have been intimately connected with brewing for

87

a very long time. The intricacies of growing hops for this purpose are fascinating, with attractive varietal names like 'Fuggles', steeped in history, but now overtaken by modern varieties such as 'Wye Challenger' that yield flower heads bursting with the phenolic lupulin for which the brewer yearns — and pays.

This, however, is all a far cry from the purpose of the hops described here, a couple of decorative varieties suitable for fence screening but for little else. The golden-leaved variety of our native hop, *H. lupulus* 'Aureus', has greenish-yellow palmate leaves. *Humulus japonica* has the similar five- to seven-lobed palmate leaf; in the variety 'Lutescens' this is a bronzy gold, and in 'Variegatus' a light spotted variegation. All are herbaceous perennials, the tops dying down to ground level and growing again with rapidity in spring. To assess the plant's coverage capacity look at any hop garden in July! American zoning is probably 5, and propagation is by division.

## *Hydrangea* (Hydrangeaceae)

We think mostly of hydrangeas in terms of stately pink and blue bushes or forced and carefully nurtured pot plants. Consequently the climbing hydrangea, *H. petiolaris*, comes as a source of surprise; it and the allied *Schizophragma* (*see* p. 144) are true climbers, however, and very useful plants for north or east walls.

*Hydrangea petiolaris* bears roundish ovate leaves, slightly and very regularly toothed, and typical hydrangea-type, plate-like corymbs of rather insignificant white flowers that have stamens and stigmas but no petals. The attractions for pollinating insects and the gardener are the few four-petalled white sterile flowers held on stalks at the edges of the 'plate'; these persist and in fact fade to a not unattractive buff-brown. The plant climbs like ivy by means of quite tough rootlets and one might assume that a piece of stem with these rootlets would, like ivy, root easily; but this is not so and the plant is not easy to propagate. Summer cuttings of half-ripened shoots in gentle heat is the usual practice.

Introduced from Japan in 1878 where it is a tree climber and reaches 60 to 80 ft (18–24 m), it will attain 30 to 40 ft (9–12 m) on house walls or trees in Britain. It is of course deciduous, the leaves assuming a lovely soft golden yellow before they fall. It is hardy enough in Britain and Zone 5 in the USA, but for sheer garden effect the rather similar *Schizophragma* is probably the better plant.

## *Ipomoea* (Convolvulaceae)

Climbing and wall plants are mostly shrubby or perennial but there are several annuals which can greatly enhance the flowering display. *Ipomoea rubro-caerulea*, the well-known 'Morning Glory', is one of these, and its soft blue, trumpet-shaped flowers have an ethereal beauty not easily described. As the common name suggests, the flowers last for the morning only; opening as the sun rises they fade around 3 o'clock but are produced in such profusion that from July to autumn every morning brings a fresh display.

The plant needs to be greenhouse-raised, seed sown in compost in April, pricked out into pots and planted out when danger of frost is past. Use it to scramble up and into other climbers or wall plants, but remember that the immediate vicinity of any shrub is occupied by its own roots seeking out moisture and nourishment. Plant it therefore where its roots are without competition, then steer the quick-growing, twining stems into the host plant by means of a light cane. Almost any shrub or climber serves as a vehicle; the grey leaves of *Cytisus battandieri* make a good background, and the combination with the yellow flowers of *Fremontodendron* is obvious but still very lovely. Autumn frosts will destroy the plant and its stems which can then be removed from the host.

The plant is known and seed is sold as *Ipomoea rubro-caerulea*, but according to the *RHS Dictionary of Gardening* it is in fact *Pharbitis tricolor*. Taxonomically I have no doubt this is correct but I have used the older name, the name under which it was superbly illustrated in *Curtis's Botanic Magazine* (t.3297) in 1834. The text accompanying the plate states that seeds were collected and sent to Britain by a Mr Samuel Richardson, 'an officer in the Anglo-Mexican Mining Association', from the province of Guanaxuate in Mexico.

89

## *Itea* (Escalloniaceae) (29)

Shrubs that prefer north walls are not very numerous; good reason then to plant *Itea ilicifolia*. Evergreen, deeply-toothed ovate leaves make a pleasant backing for the shower of pendulous tassels, each 6 to 10 in (15 to 25 cm) long, crowded with small greenish-white flowers that are produced in August. It is not a climber and requires only the occasional tie to keep it to the sheltering wall that it needs in most parts of Britain. A border some 3 to 4 ft (90 to 120 cm) wide should be allowed for its ultimate development. Pruning other than to control spread is unnecessary; propagation is by cuttings of half-ripened wood. It was introduced by seed sent from its native Western China by the plant collector, Dr Augustine Henry (1857–1930) and first flowered in 1895. Often said to be tender it is, in my experience, best on a protected north wall rather than in warmer spots where the early morning sun plays havoc with frozen leaves. In the USA it is unlikely to succeed in Zones below 8.

## *Jasminum* (Oleaceae)

The Jasmines, summer and winter, together with 'Japonica' (*Chaenomeles*) and rambler roses, are artists' favourite adornments to picturesque cottage pictures. It is true to say that they are often grown as wall plants although they do not need protection but do need support. The winter-flowering *Jasminum nudiflorum* (30), blooming from November to February, is probably the most appreciated. Hard frosts may destroy its open flowers but a few days of mild weather will garland the bare twigs with primrose-like, bright yellow flowers. A native of China, it was introduced in 1844 by the plant explorer Robert Fortune (1812–80). In 1842 the Treaty of Nanking had been signed opening up a number of Chinese ports to the British. The Horticultural Society, later (1861) to become the Royal Horticultural Society, realised the wealth of new plants that might be found in China and appointed Robert Fortune, at that time Superintendent of their hot houses, as their plant collector in

China. Fortune proved a very able collector and *Jasminum nudiflorum* was one of the many fine plants he introduced. Of more economic importance perhaps was his skill in passing himself as a Chinese and obtaining tea plants (*Camellia thea*) and the secrets of tea cultivation for the East India Company. He was thus the founder of the great tea industry of India.

*Jasminum nudiflorum* is not naturally a climber and will initially require some form of support and tying. Pruning is often confined to overall clipping back and this it seems to survive; a more proper system (although laborious) is to cut out the old flowered wood and any shoots that have died back, immediately after flowering.

Its summer counterpart, *J. officinale*, a native of Persia, the Caucasus and Afghanistan, has been an occupant of British gardens for so long that its date of introduction is not known. Bearing trusses of white, fragrant flowers from July onwards, the plant makes a tangle of growth. No pruning other than that required to keep it within bounds is needed. It is a most suitable climber for covering summer houses or other garden structures. If planted as a wall climber it is best in the shade and will need a lattice of wood or wire to aid the upward progress of the long young growths. It drops its leaves in severe weather and although generally hardy in Britain needs wall protection in the north and doubtless in many parts of the USA. The form sold as 'Affine' has larger flowers and is well worth seeking, the cultivar 'Aureum' has bright yellow leaf variegation but in such a plant this is not, in my opinion, an improvement.

Another summer-flowering kind which could be planted more extensively is *J. x stephanense*, the 'Pink Jasmine'. This hybrid between *J. beesianum*, a not very floriferous red-flowered species, and *J. officinale* was put into commerce by the Lemoine Nursery at Nancy in France in 1921. In habit and time of flowering it is similar to *J. officinale* but is slightly less vigorous; the fragrant flowers are soft pink.

These Jasmines are readily propagated by cuttings of semi-ripe wood taken in late summer, indeed the long growths particularly those of *J. nudiflorum* root readily when in contact with the soil making natural layers. The name *Jasminum*, popularly 'Jasmine' is said to be derived from *Ysmyn*, the Arabic name for the plant.

## *Kadsura* (Schisandraceae)

Interesting but rarely grown, *K. japonica*, formerly placed with the magnolias in Magnoliaceae, can only be grown outside as a wall plant in mild areas, Zone 7 in the USA. A twining evergreen up to 12 ft (3.5 m) it has lanceolate, dark green leaves and inconspicuous white flowers, about $\frac{3}{4}$ in (2 cm) across, borne from June through to the autumn. *Kadsura* is reputedly monoecious, that is male and female flowers are borne on the same plant, so in reasonable seasons globose clusters of scarlet berries, the plant's only attraction, should result. The sheltered wall that it requires can, however, be used for more garden-worthy plants. Native to China, Japan and Formosa and introduced in 1860, it may be propagated by summer cuttings set in sand in a warm frame.

## *Kerria* (Rosaceae) (31)

A familiar and delightful cottage shrub, *Kerria japonica* 'Pleniflora', the 'Jew's Mallow', does not need protection but looks so much better against a wall. The light-green, cane-like stems spring from a suckering rootstock making it an easy plant to propagate. In April and May they carry generous clusters of egg-yolk yellow, double flowers with a background of light green leaves. It will grow in almost any soil but is less happy on peaty or thin dry soils. For pruning it is sufficient for canes that have flowered to be cut out at ground level during the summer. Looking well against red-brick it is hardy enough to flourish against north and east walls and inhospitable positions. In the USA a Zone 5 plant; in colder areas zero frosts can destroy canes to ground level.

The generic name honours William Kerr, a young Kew gardener who was sent out to collect in China. He found the plant growing in Chinese gardens and sent it back in 1804. The wild single form was not discovered until 1834; it is more bushy and although not without beauty is not suited as a wall plant.

## *Laburnum* (Leguminosae)

Laburnum (how easily we use its proper Latin botanical name!) is neither climber or wall plant but appears here by virtue of the

1 *Abutilon ochsenii*

2 *Abutilon megapotamicum*          3 *Abutilon vitifolium*

4 *Actinidia kolomikta*

5 *Aristolochia sempervirens*

6 *Buddleia colvilei* 'Kewensis'

7  Caesalpinia sepiaria

8  Callistemon salignus

9  Carpenteria californica

10  Ceanothus dentatus

11 *Celastrus orbiculatus*

12 *Cestrum* 'Newellii'

13 *Chimonanthus praecox*

14 *Clematis montana* 'Rubens' on *Thuja plicata*

15 *Clematis* 'Henryi'

16 *Clematis* 'Barbara Dibley'

17 *Clematis* 'Perle d'Azure'

18 *Clematis orientalis*

19 *Clematis* 'Nelly Moser'

20 *Clianthus puniceus*

21 *Cobaea scandens*

22 *Cotoneaster horizontalis* 'Variegata'

23 *Cytisus battandieri*

24 *Forsythia x intermedia* 'Spectabilis'

25 *Fremontodendron* 'California Glory'

26 *Garrya elliptica*

27 *Hedera colchica* 'Sulphur Heart'

28 *Hoheria sexstylosa*

29 *Itea ilicifolia*

30 *Jasminum nudiflorum*

31 *Kerria japonica* 'Pleniflora'

32 *Laburnum x watereri* 'Vossii'

33 *Lathyrus rotundifolius*                    34 *Leptospermum scoparium*

35 *Lonicera periclymenum* 'Graham Thomas'

36 *Passiflora caerulea*

37 *Phlomis fruticosa*

38 *Pyracantha* 'Mohave'

39 *Robinia hispida*

40 *Rosa* 'Climbing Cecile Brunner'

41 *Rosa* 'Helen Knight' and *Clematis montana* 'Tetrarose'

42 *Rosa* 'Complicata'

43 *Rosa* 'Golden Showers'

44 *Rosa* 'Schoolgirl'

45 *Teucrium fruticans*

46 *Tropaeolum speciosum*

47 *Wisteria floribunda* 'Alba'

48 *Wisteria sinensis*

occasional but rewarding practice of training specimens in the form of an archway. The technique is described on page 18 and plate **32** depicts an example at Hampton Court. The best cultivar for the purpose is *Laburnum x watereri* 'Vossii', one of the named forms of the cross between *L. alpinum* and *L. anagyroides*. Raised in Holland late in the nineteenth century, it is floriferous and in the length of its racemes of golden yellow flowers exceeds all others.

Laburnum is of course hardy in Britain and down to Zone 5 in the USA, but late spring frosts can sometimes destroy the unopened flower buds, a slight gamble worth taking to enjoy this loveliest and most graceful of yellow-flowering trees. Both species have been grown in Britain for so long that the date of introduction from their native central and southern Europe is not known. The species are propagated by seed, hybrids by grafting or budding. Interestingly, as with so many yellow-flowered shrubs, there is no record of a white form.


## *Lagerstroemia* (Lythraceae)

With care and winter cover a 'Crape Myrtle', *L. indica*, is reported to have survived and flowered out of doors in the USA as far north as Philadelphia although its more likely Zone is 6. This lovely shrub needs the hot summers of continental climates and it is this rather than winter cold that is the limiting factor. In some years it flowers well in Sussex and if protection can be given in winter months it may do best in high sunshine areas of eastern England but of course will need to be on a south wall.

A deciduous shrub with privet-like leaves, it grows quickly and seedlings are said to flower in their second year. When established hard pruning is necessary to encourage the production of sturdy current year's shoots. In hot summers these terminate, from July to September, in panicles up to 9 in (22 cm) long of charming, 1 in (2.5 cm) wide, crinkle petalled, light pink flowers. There is a rose-pink form, 'Rosea', and the white 'Alba'. Propagated by seed or by cuttings of ripened shoots taken in August or September and inserted in sand/peat in a warm propagating frame. A native of China and Korea, it was introduced to Kew in 1759.

## Lapageria (Philesiaceae)

Like *Philesia, Lapageria rosea* in Britain is a risk plant and only possible out of doors in mild climatically-favoured areas; in the USA a Zone 9 plant. It needs a warm wall position but with shade during the hottest part of the day. A lime-free soil with plenty of humus and moisture are its other requirements.

It is an evergreen twining climber to some 10 or 12 ft (3–3.5 m) with heart-shaped leaves, leathery in texture and pendulous six-petalled, bell-shaped, soft-crimson flowers, thick and waxy to the touch. In its native Chile from where it was introduced in 1847 there are several colour variations between crimson and the white 'Albiflora'. In Britain it flowers from mid-summer to autumn. Propagation is by means of seed or layering during spring or autumn.

It is interesting in that the monotypic genus to which it belongs was named to honour the first wife of Napoleon Bonaparte, Empress Josephine of France whose maiden name was Josephine de la Pagerie.

## Lardizabala biternata (Lardizabalaceae)

A rather tender plant but worth trying on sheltered walls in mild districts. It forms a vigorous, leafy climber, the tough evergreen leaves having two or often three ovate leaflets. The flowers are unisexual and on separate plants. The male flowers produced in drooping spikes 3 to 4 in (7.5–10 cm) long are each about $\frac{3}{4}$ in (1.5 cm) across with prominent fleshy, chocolate-coloured sepals, the small white petals looking more like stamens. The female flowers are larger but solitary and borne in the leaf axils. If the plants are growing well, sausage-shaped, dark purple, edible fruits will be produced. The plant was introduced from Chile to Messrs Veitch of Exeter in 1844 by William Lobb (1809–63) who noted that the fruit was sold in the Chilean markets. The plant can be propagated by seed sown in a heated greenhouse or by cuttings of young shoots in sand under a bell glass within a frame in July or August. A Zone 8 or 9 plant in the USA.

## *Lathyrus* (Leguminosae)

This genus includes the Sweet Pea, *L. odoratus*, one of the best known of all climbing plants. An annual too well known to need description, it is not always easy to place in the garden. For producing flowers for cutting it is hard to beat a row across the garden grown on pea-sticks; equally they can be grown as clumps within a border of annuals. For the purposes of this book they can be used to fill in the sides of pergolas, interspersed perhaps with other plants. They are not well suited to grow against walls or fences and if scrambling through shrubs can look somewhat artificial.

Several species, however, escape this accusation and being strong growers can provide colour in places to which more difficult plants may object. *Lathyrus latifolius*, often seen in cottage gardens, is just such a plant; completely hardy, it has carmine-red flowers from July onwards. There is a good white form *L. latifolius* 'Albus' and cultivars 'Snow Queen', 'Roseus' (a bright rose-pink) and 'Splendens', a large-flowered form. The white and rose forms planted together create a very good effect.

*Lathyrus pubescens* from the Argentine is an attractive plant with lilac-blue flowers, and as it is slightly tender it needs the protection of a south wall. The Persian Everlasting Pea, *L. rotundifolius* (**33**), a native of Eastern Europe, is hardy, not as tall growing as *L. latifolius* and with rosy-red flowers. All may be raised from seed and the three perennial species by division of rooted clumps. Zones 5–6 in the USA, except *L. pubescens* (Zone 7).

## *Leonotis* (Labiatae)

The 'Lion's Ear' is a little known plant that in Britain can make a sub-shrub given a south or west wall in the mildest of areas. Where it can be grown it is particularly welcome on account of its late October to November flowering period.

The common name is derived from a fanciful resemblance of the corolla to a lion's ear; not being familiar with lions nor with their ears I am unable to confirm this. *Leonotis leonurus* was introduced to Britain from its native South Africa in 1712 as a

111

CLIMBERS AND WALL PLANTS

plant for the greenhouse. The stems are square, the leaves oblong-lanceolate, soft green and slightly downy. The typically labiate 'dead-nettle' flowers are large, up to 2 in (5 cm) long, borne in whorls and of bright orange-scarlet. A good loam soil, a mild climate and a fine autumn are its requirements. No doubt a Zone 9 plant in the USA.


## *Leptospermum* (Myrtaceae)

A genus of Australian and New Zealand shrubs that require wall protection in most parts of Britain and preferably an acid soil. The best and most commonly planted species is *L. scoparium* (**34**), the 'Manuka' or 'Tea Plant' of New Zealand. An evergreen wall plant that will grow to 3 or 4 ft (1–1.2 m), the rather twiggy stems are clad with small, sharply-pointed leaves that are fragrant when crushed and in late spring covered profusely with $\frac{1}{2}$ to $\frac{3}{4}$ in (1–1.5 cm), five petalled flowers. Of the many varieties available, 'Nicholsii', crimson with bronzy purple leaves is probably the best known. It originated from a single plant found on a sheep run north of Christchurch, New Zealand, from where seed was obtained and from which the plant was propagated, it was introduced to Britain in 1908. Other good varieties are: 'Album Flore Pleno', the double white; 'Boscawenii', bright rose; 'Keatleyi', large-flowered soft pink; and 'Roseum Multipetalum', double rose-pink. 'Red Damask', a very fine double red, was raised in the 1930s by Dr Lammerts of the University of California; close-growing and very free-flowering, it is the best red. A Zone 8 plant in USA. In my experience no pruning is necessary, and it is propagated by means of semi-ripe small cuttings inserted in sand/peat in a cold frame in late summer.


## *Lippia* (Verbenaceae)

Anyone considering plants for sheltered walls must give thought to, should indeed procure, a plant of *L. citriodora*, the 'Lemon Scented Verbena'. It is a modest plant taking up little enough room and boasting nothing in the way of floral attraction. A plant to place in a sheltered corner handy to a pathway so that you may crush a leaf in your hand as you pass and savour the lovely pure lemon fragrance. A plant for a sheltered nook on a walled terrace or patio.

In such a favourable spot it will form a slender deciduous shrub up to 6 ft (1.8 m) high, bearing light green, lanceolate, rather soft leaves with veins notably parallel to the midrib. The leaves are disposed in threes at each node of the shoots which terminate in August in spikes about 4 in (10 cm) long of small pale lilac to white flowers. The younger growth is easily cut back by frost but once a woody stem is established it should, in a sheltered spot, persist and grow well enough. It is easily propagated by summer cuttings inserted in sandy soil in a cold frame. A Zone 8 plant in the USA, it used to be a favourite cottage-window pot plant in Britain (where it was introduced from Chile via Spain in 1784 as *Aloysia citriodora*, under which name it is sometimes still listed).

## *Lonicera* (Caprifoliaceae)

Talk of climbing plants and people's thoughts usually turn to honeysuckle, for although roses and clematis may steal the limelight few flowering climbers are better loved than members of this family, in particular perhaps our own woodbine, *Lonicera periclymenum*.

With the help of trellis, honeysuckles can be trained on walls, but they are better and more attractive over small trees, or covering pergolas, balconies or summer houses. Woodland plants preferring shade and reasonable moisture at the root, they will thrust their heads into the sunshine. The following summary contains some well known favourites as well as a few that deserve to be more widely planted.

### *L. x americana*
The result of a cross between *L. caprifolium* and *L. etrusca* made before 1750, it is an old inhabitant of gardens yet still not planted as frequently as it warrants. A vigorous climber, the fragrant white flowers, $1\frac{1}{2}$ to 2 in (4 to 5 cm) long, age to deep yellow; profusely borne, they make a superb July display.

113

### L. x brownii

Another cross, this one between *L. hirsuta* and *L. sempervirens*. Often semi-evergreen, moderately vigorous, leaves are downy, glaucous beneath and often perfoliate. The flowers 1 to $1\frac{1}{2}$ in (2.5 to 4 cm) long and borne in whorls, are rich orange scarlet but lack scent. Several clones of the cross are in circulation; the best is 'Dropmore Scarlet'.

### L. etrusca

Introduced from the Mediterranean area around 1750, this is a plant for the drier and sunnier parts of Britain. Fragrant cream-coloured flowers $1\frac{1}{2}$ in (4 cm) long, deepening to yellow with age. A vigorous plant that is usually deciduous under British conditions.

### L. japonica

The form of this Japanese plant most commonly grown, and certainly the best, is *L. japonica* 'Halliana'. Introduced to American nurseries by Dr George Hall in 1862 and often called 'Hall's Honeysuckle', it did not in fact reach British gardens until the 1880s. Flowering from June to early October it is semi-evergreen, quick-growing and excellent cover for pergolas, summer houses, sheds or trees. The soft, hairy leaves produce in their axils pairs of fragrant, cream-coloured flowers, ageing to buff, that give the plant an attractive two-colour appearance. A good natured plant for virtually any soil, it withstands pruning to keep it within bounds, a task best done in early spring. In the eastern USA it displays rampant energy and is almost a pest, but in Britain is invaluable for its sweetly scented coverage. Not a good wall climber where it has a tendency to make a too bulky overhanging top.

### L. periclymenum

Loveliest of British wild plants, and the 'luscious woodbine' depicted by Oberon in Shakespeare's *Midsummer Night's Dream*. A vigorous climber, a woodland plant with white delicately fragrant flowers; an informal plant seen at its best in the shade of oaks and the wild garden. A particularly good form 'Graham Thomas' **(35)**, floriferous and with slightly broader petals, is in existence and worth seeking. For situations nearer the house, on hedge, fence, shed, summer house or pergola, plant the form 'Belgica', the so-called 'Early Dutch Honeysuckle', with May and June flowers, red-purple on the outside ageing to buff-yellow, or 'Serotina', the 'Late Dutch', flowering in July and of similar colour. Both flower more profusely than the British native and are equally fragrant, but being more formal in appearance are more suited to the uses I have described.

## L. sempervirens

The 'Trumpet Honeysuckle', which is usually semi-evergreen with glaucous green leaves and rich orange scarlet flowers, $1\frac{1}{2}$ to 2 in (4 to 5 cm) long in summer. A native of the eastern USA, it has been grown in Britain since 1656, but is best treated as a wall plant. It is unscented.

## L. standishii

This shrub honeysuckle is perfectly hardy and there is no reason to grow it against a wall other than to provide protection for the fragrant, cream-coloured flowers produced at the nodes of the bare twigs from January to March. Introduced from China by Robert Fortune in 1845 and welcome for its early flowers.

## L. x tellmanniana

Another cross, this time between *L. sempervirens* and *L. tragophylla*. Raised in Hungary around 1927 it is definitely a plant for shade or semi-shade. The 2 in (5 cm) flowers of rich coppery-yellow are borne in clusters in June and July but, alas, are not fragrant.

## L. tragophylla

This too lacks scent, but again is a good shade plant. The golden-yellow flowers produced in June and July in terminal clusters are large, $2\frac{1}{2}$ to $3\frac{1}{2}$ in (6 to 9 cm) long. From Western China it was introduced by Ernest Wilson (1876–1930), sometime Keeper of the Arnold Arboretum in America and known as 'Chinese Wilson' from his very successful plant hunting trips in China.

All these honeysuckles are readily propagated by cuttings of half-ripened wood taken in July and inserted in sandy compost in a closed frame. In the USA they are generally Zone 5 plants.

115

## *Magnolia* (Magnoliaceae)

With one exception magnolias are not really wall plants, and for the exception, M. *grandiflora*, a large building, two storeys or more, is necessary. This magnolia was widely planted towards the end of the last century and fine specimens can still be seen up and down the country, often on walls of the large rectories and vicarages of Victorian days.

Although wall protection is not essential, its evergreen habit, magnificent glossy medium-green leaves and stature make it an impressive adjunct to a large house, although some years may pass before it bears its massive globular, spicily fragrant white flowers. In the cultivar 'Goliath' these are up to a foot (30 cm) across, and as in the species produced throughout the summer. First sent out by the Caledonia Nursery of Guernsey, it is the finest of the several varieties in existence. Propagated by layers or cuttings M. *grandiflora* is not a lime-lover but likes and deserves a good deep loam. Introduced from the southern USA early in the eighteenth century.

## *Mandevilla* (Apocynaceae)

The planting outside of M. *suaveolens*, the 'Chilean Jasmine', must in Britain be confined to the south and west and in America to Zone 9 areas. It is a deciduous twining climber with cordate-oblong, dark green leaves, and bearing in summer white, gloriously fragrant five-petalled flowers. Introduced from the Argentine in 1837, there are favourable areas where given a fairly rich peaty soil it could be successfully grown. Propagated by summer cuttings in gentle heat. Like many members of its family the stems when cut exude a milky juice. The generic name honours Mr H. J. Mandeville, at that time British Minister in Buenos Aires, who introduced the species to Britain.

## *Menispermum* (Menispermaceae)

The 'Moonseed', M. *canadense*, is seldom grown in Britain but is of some interest by reason of the single crescent or moon-shaped

116

seed contained in each of the small blackcurrant-like fruits borne in loose trusses following fertilisation of the female flowers; the plant is monoecious, i.e. male and female flowers are present on the one plant. It is vigorous, extending to 12 or 15 ft (3.5–4.5 m) and suitable for growing over trees, sheds etc in full sun; likely to be cut down to the ground in cold winters, it grows away again rapidly in spring. The flowers are greenish-yellow and inconspicuous, the 4 to 7 in (10–18 cm) deciduous leaves peltate in shape. A native of eastern North America, a Zone 5 plant, it was introduced to Britain in the seventeenth century. It spreads rapidly by underground stems and is thus easily propagated.

## *Mimulus aurantiacus* (Scrophulariaceae)

*Mimulus* are usually annuals or herbaceous plants, but this is one of the few woody species. At one time these were placed in a separate genus *Diplacus*, this species being *D. glutinosus* under which name it is still sometimes seen. A native of California, it was possibly introduced into Britain by Archibald Menzies (1754–1842) late in the eighteenth century.

Seldom exceeding 3 ft (90 cm) in height, it is evergreen, the narrow leaves dark green above and glutinous. The light-orange flowers are of typical *Mimulus* structure and have an interesting sensitive stigma; this is seen as a white, two-lipped structure like a small flap on the upper side inside the 'throat' of the flower. The interest arises in that when lightly touched with finger or a matchstick the two lips close together rapidly, the purpose being to preclude self-fertilisation. The bee entering and seeking nectar and thereby transferring the flower's pollen on to its body will not, on its retreat, transfer it to the stigma since its entry has caused the lips to close together, receiving from the bee pollen from a neighbouring flower. This ensures cross-pollination but excludes self-fertilisation, an interesting plant stratagem and an amusing party trick for garden visitors.

A delightful little plant, with wall protection it is reasonably hardy in Britain; its US limit is probably Zone 8. Easily propagated by cuttings, it is prudent to have a few plants in reserve in case hard winters prevail; the cuttings flower at an early stage. A red form sometimes called *M. puniceus* is in cultivation, but is less pleasant than the orange form.

117

## Mitraria (Gesneriaceae)

The single species that constitutes this genus, *M. coccinea*, is a lovely low climber and a challenge to the gardener's skill. Introduced in 1846 by William Lobb (1809–63), plant collecting for Messrs Veitch of Exeter, it comes from the Maulé province of Chile — an area of very high rainfall. Successful cultivation requires a lime-free, moist soil, partial shade and an equable moist climate such as is experienced in the west of Britain. The reward of success is a plant with evergreen, opposite, rather leathery, bluntly-toothed ovate leaves and during July a succession of rich scarlet, yellow-throated, tubular flowers that have the slightly pouchy appearance often characteristic of Gesneriad flowers. Probably a Zone 8 plant in the USA and, as in Britain, dependent on a moist micro-climate. It can be propagated by cuttings of young shoots in sand under a bell glass in a frame during summer; division of the roots during spring is also possible.

## Mutisia (Compositae)

Unfortunately the best of the 'Climbing Gazanias' of South America is not in cultivation at the present time; this is, or was, *Mutisia decurrens*, a lovely scrambling climber with large vivid orange daisy flowers. One consolation, perhaps, is that when it has been available to gardeners it has always proved extremely difficult to cultivate.

Two species of this interesting family that are available and can be grown outside are *M. ilicifolia* and *M. oligodon*. They need a south or west aspect and are best planted where they can scramble into accommodating bushy wall plants. Failing this some fairly robust pea sticks placed against the wall will enable the leaves, which have an extended mid-rib developed into a tendril, to get a hold and secure the plant. The leaves are greyish-green with slightly toothed edges. The flowers, about 2 to 3 in (5–7.5 cm) across, have prominent yellow 'daisy' centres surrounded in the case of *M. ilicifolia* with lilac-pink, and in *M. ologodon*, salmon-pink, petals. The latter is probably the better plant being more compact in habit although in winter they can

118

both look rather like collections of dead stems. They are natives of Chile, *M. ilicifolia* introduced in 1832, and *M. oligodon*, although known and described earlier, not introduced until 1927 when it was collected by Harold Comber (1897–1969). They are suckering plants and it is said that the production of suckers on which the plant's renewal depends is encouraged by placing flat stones around the roots. It is fair to say that these are plants of interest and rarity rather than outstanding beauty. Propagated by seed or cuttings of half-ripened shoots taken in July or August and placed in a close sand-frame in heat. They are probably vigorous climbers in the southern USA (Zones 8–9).

## *Osmanthus* (Oleaceae)

Evergreen shrubs with white, mostly fragrant flowers, *Osmanthus* will flourish in the open in Britain. One species, however, *O. delavayii*, is particularly acceptable as a wall plant, the more so since its hardiness recommends it as a north wall plant (although listed Zone 6 in the USA).

An evergreen with small, closely set, dark-green leaves, it bears in April along and at the ends of its branches clusters of small, $\frac{1}{2}$ in (1 cm), white, fragrant flowers. Backed by the dark green leafage the effect is lovely, the shrub often almost hidden by the wealth of flower. It is rather slow-growing but will do well on chalk soils and as a wall plant probably appreciates the residue of lime associated with house walls. It is propagated by summer cuttings of half-ripened wood and requires no pruning but will stand shortening back if it outgrows its station. A native of China, it was introduced by J. M. Delavay (1834–95), the French missionary who in 1890 sent seed to the Paris School of Arboriculture.

## *Paeonia* (Paeoniaceae)

In one's imagination the sumptuous flowers of the Tree Peony, large, fragrant and colourful, suggest the need of a warm sheltered position; in fact the reverse is true. The plant is very hardy and is best planted against a north wall. If excited into

119

early growth by being in too warm a situation the flower buds can be killed by late spring frosts; because of this they do better in northern and eastern Britain. In the south they are best planted against a north-facing wall, preferably a draughty corner which can be a defence against *Botrytis paeoniae*, the fungus which causes peony wilt and is encouraged by warm humid conditions. This apart they ask only for a deep rich soil, a good loam well manured before planting, and although lime tolerant they grow perfectly well on acid soils.

The plant is widely grown in the United States where leading growers list hundreds of varieties. In Britain some of the best, among which are the following, need to be sought from the few nurserymen specialising in these lovely plants. 'Argosy', a large single yellow; 'Bijou de Chusan', fine double white; 'Chromatella', large double sulphur-yellow; 'Comtesse de Tuder', a double blush-pink; 'Jeanne d'Arc', fine double pink with a darker centre; 'Mme Louis Henry', yellow suffused red; 'Red Brocade', semi-double carmine with gold centre; 'Reine Elisabeth', double crimson; and the superb 'Souvenir de Maxime Cornu', massively double, light brownish orange and red.

These garden varieties were derived principally from two species, *Paeonia lutea*, discovered in Yunnan by the French missionary Jean Marie Delavay in 1887, and *P. suffruticosa*, cultivated in China for centuries and introduced to Britain by Sir Joseph Banks in 1787. A variety of *P. lutea*, found in southeastern Tibet by the botanical expedition of Frank Ludlow and Major George Sheriff in 1936 and known as var. *ludlowii*, has single, yellow cup-shaped flowers 4 to 5 in (10–13 cm) across. Making a rather upright bush 6 to 8 ft (1.5–2.5 m) high, it is usually raised from seed, and plants can vary somewhat. At its best it is a very lovely plant.

## *Parthenocissus* (Vitaceae)

The popular Virginia creeper, a native of America, was introduced as long ago as 1629. One of Britain's finest climbing plants the early writers assumed it to be a kind of ivy and we find it listed as '*Hedera canadensis scandens*' in the *Universal Botanist and Nurseryman* published in 1770. There are a number of species and varieties. The following are the most common and probably the most useful.

### P. henryana

Leaves of velvety green lightly marked white along the veins, the green part turning a glorious red in autumn, make this a flower arranger's plant and the doyen of the genus. A native of Central China, it was discovered by the explorer Augustine Henry around 1885 but not introduced into Britain until 1900. It clings in the same manner as the better known *P. tricuspidata* and requires the shelter of a wall, but will thrive and indeed show its discreet white markings better on north or north-west walls.

### P. quinquefolia

This is the true 'Virginia creeper' that was introduced from Eastern North America in 1629. The leaves are usually five-lobed and more regular than in *P. tricuspidata*. It is rarely seen or planted now, its place having been taken over by the closer growing *P. tricuspidata*, a plant coming from Japan and with no American or Virginian connections.

### P. tricuspidata

This is the 'Boston Ivy'. In Britain often erroneously termed 'Virginia creeper', it was introduced from Japan by the nursery firm of Veitch in 1862. The leaves are variable, three- or five-lobed, toothed, and bright light green. The most commonly planted species and often sold under its earlier names of *Ampelopsis veitchii* or *Vitis inconstans*, it is an excellent wall climber, successful on north or east walls, and like the other *Parthenocissus* a Zone 5 plant in USA. By reason of its vigour it is suitable only for high walls or houses of more than one storey. Once planted no treatment is required save clipping back in mid-summer if it proves invasive of gutters or windows. An outstanding example of its power of coverage may be seen on the massive concrete-formed 'War Room' adjacent to Admiralty Arch in London. This prominent reminder of the dark days of World War 2 is covered with a close mat of this species, in summer completely softening the severity of the building. Being deciduous it loses its leaves in autumn, albeit in a blaze of red and orange autumn colour, but even in winter the mat of fine stems helps to blur the harshness of the building.

121

## *Passiflora caerulea* (Passifloraceae) (36)

There are a number of species of Passion Flower, among them *Passiflora edulis* which provides the Passion Fruit of commerce. Fortunately *P. caerulea* is sufficiently hardy to adorn south-facing walls in sheltered parts of Britain. In the USA it will not, apart from in the southern states, survive outside, but is recommended as a greenhouse vine or climber. Likewise in the colder areas of Britain it is an excellent plant for the unheated greenhouse.

The colloquial name of 'Passion Flower' was given by Spanish priests, in the plant's native Brazil, who saw in the elaborate flower structure a resemblance to the elements of Christ's Passion. The three stigmas represented the three nails, two for the hands and one for the feet; the five anthers the five wounds; the corona, the conspicuous ring of thread-like growths, the Crown of Thorns. The five sepals and five petals stand for the ten apostles, Peter and Judas being absent, and the tendrils and hand-like leaves represent the whips and hands of Christ's persecutors.

Easily propagated by seeds or cuttings, the plant is not difficult to cultivate — it only requires a good deep soil. It is worth covering the base of the stem for some 18 in (45 cm) to 2 ft (60 cm) with a light covering of hay or bracken in the first few winters of the plant's life. Once established it climbs vigorously supporting itself by tendrils and producing a mass of more or less evergreen five-lobed leaves. The showy five-petalled blue flowers backed by light green sepals are flat and open, slightly fragrant and produced from July until the autumn frosts. The ovoid, orange-coloured fruits are sometimes produced during warm summers; they are edible but not recommended as a culinary delight.

The foliage, although evergreen, often looks tatty at winter's end but the plant is well worth trying in the Home Counties and sheltered sites elsewhere. A native of Brazil reputedly introduced in 1609, it is beautiful, interesting and a very worth while wall climber. The cultivar 'Constance Elliott' has ivory-white flowers but in all other respects is the same as the species. It was introduced in 1884.

## *Periploca* (Periplocaceae)

The Silk Vine, *Periploca graeca*, is a twining climber that grows rapidly and covers itself with lustrous dark green, ovate leaves. Plant it with caution, for it is virtually indestructible. Good cover for an unsightly building or dead tree, it is, however, deciduous, making it a less effective screen than ivy if winter cover is required. The flowers are small, about 1 in (2.5 cm) across, brownish-purple and not very noticeable. The seed pods are in pairs, about 5 in (12 cm) long but joined at the tips and looking rather like a pair of pincers. Leaves and stems if cut exude a white juice that is poisonous. Propagated by seed or division, any reasonably fertile soil and a sunny situation are all that it requires. As might be expected from a plant hailing from the Balkans and near East it is hardy in Britain and above Zone 5 in the USA. The genus was formerly included in Asclepiadaceae but botanical revision has given it a family of its own.

## *Perovskia* (Labiatae)

Introduced from Afghanistan in 1904 and needing the sunniest position possible, *P. atriplicifolia* is a good wall plant and suitable as a screen plant to hide the bare lower stems of wall climbers; for this purpose it is best planted as a group of three or four plants. From a perennial rootstock semi-woody stems 3 to 4 ft (90–120 cm) tall are produced, foliaged with grey-green leaves and terminating in August–September in panicled heads of small violet-blue flowers surrounded with dense white down. The cultivar 'Blue Spire' has much larger panicles of flower and is the best form to plant.

Although hardy over most of Britain, probably Zone 7 in the USA, some growth is invariably cut back by winter frosts; this dead wood should be pruned back in spring. The plant is propagated by cuttings of young wood taken in June. The generic name honours V. A. Perovski, a provincial governor in Russia at the time (1841) that the genus was established.

## *Philadelphus* (Saxifragaceae)

Well known as one of the loveliest of fragrant shrubs for the border or as a lawn specimen, the 'Mock Orange' or 'Syringa' is rarely seen as a wall shrub. The taller kinds, however, which make long arching stems can be so used even against north or east walls providing the wall height is not less than 12 ft (3.5 m); in this position the lovely scent of the white June to July flowers can be appreciated from upstairs windows.

To use the plant successfully in this way regular pruning out of the flowered stems immediately after flowering is essential, the young current year's shoots being then tied in to the wall. The most commonly planted species, *P. coronarius*, a native of south-east Europe and Asia Minor, is one of the oldest and best-loved shrubs of our gardens. Gerard, the herbalist, cultivated it in 1597 and commented on the almost overpowering sweetness of its scent which indoors he described as 'troubling and molesting', a stricture with which I personally cannot agree. More vigorous and equally suitable for wall planting is *P.* 'Virginal' with fine double flowers and scent that is not quite so penetrating as that of *P. coronarius*. Suitable and equally lovely is the single *P. delavayi*, a native of W. China and Tibet, introduced by the Abbé Delavay in 1887; the white flowers have purple calyces particularly pronounced in a form raised from seed sent home by George Forrest (1873–1932) in the 1930s and called 'Nyman's Variety'. There is a similar clone in existence called 'Calvescens'. *P.* 'Minnesota Snowflake' and *P. intectus* are two more worth trying in a wall position. Hardy in USA Zone 5, any reasonable soil suits *Philadelphus* including fairly poor chalk soils.

## *Philesia* (Philesiaceae)

A monotypic genus, i.e. a genus having only one species, *P. magellanica* is closely allied to *Lapageria* and like it very much a risk plant in Britain, but a risk worth taking more often than it is. Generally a fairly low, 3 ft (1 m) suckering shrub making a thicket of wiry stems clad with narrow rather rigid evergreen leaves, it will in suitable conditions climb to 6 or 8 ft (1.8–2.4 m) by means of adventitious roots. The very lovely rose-crimson flowers comprise three petals encircling each other to form a tubular flower with a flared mouth. They are produced in late summer and autumn. Essential requirements for cultural success are shelter, a moist atmosphere, peaty soil and shade. A sheltered site on a north wall suits the plant admirably. In the dry conditions of eastern England it is pointless to try. A Zone 9 plant in the USA, it can be propagated by cuttings or more easily by suckers.

The plant was discovered in the Magellan region of Chile by the French naturalist Philibert Commerson. It is recorded that he was accompanied on his explorations by his mistress, Jeanne Baret, disguised as a manservant. This explains perhaps the delightful generic name so fittingly chosen by Commerson which comes from the Greek verb *philein*, 'to love'.

## *Phlomis* (Labiatae)

The 'Jerusalem Sage', *P. fruticosa* (**37**), is a good low shrub to furnish the base of a wall in dry sunny position and can usefully screen the bare lower stems of wall climbers. It forms a large sage like bush with dull-green, wrinkled, downy leaves 3 to 6 in (7.5–15 cm) long. The bright yellow labiate type flowers each 1 in (2.5 cm) or more long and interestingly hooded are borne in tight whorled clusters at the shoot ends. A native of the Mediterranean region it has been grown in Britain since the sixteenth century. If clematis of the viticella group can be planted on the north side of a wall to climb over so as to flower on the south side, above and into bushes of *Phlomis*, a very pretty picture indeed can be contrived. A plant for the drier parts of the USA, but probably confined to Zone 8 unless it can be given winter protection. Propagated by young side shoots inserted in sand in a propagating case or frame.

Two other species are sometimes seen. *P. chrysophylla* differs in being of lower stature and with slightly smaller leaves that have a golden green tinge due to the presence of numerous golden hairs, and the flowers are a slightly deeper yellow than *P. fruticosa*. The other, *P. italica*, from the Balearic islands, has pale lilac flowers and grey, somewhat woolly, leaves. Although interesting neither are such good garden plants as *P. fruticosa*.

125

## Phygelius (Scrophulariaceae)

In most parts of Britain the growth of *Phygelius*, like that of fuchsias, is cut to the ground in winter. Spring sees the emergence of stout stems clothed with dark-green, lanceolate leaves and terminating in panicles of red flowers followed by pouchy seed vessels. In *P. capensis*, the 'Cape Figwort', introduced from South Africa in 1850, the tubular, nodding flowers are scarlet with a yellow throat. The other known species, *P. aequalis*, also from South Africa, was introduced in the 1930s and is slightly less hardy. The flowers are pink on the outside and more pendulous. Both species are propagated easily from summer cuttings or by seed and are fine plants for south or west walls and well-drained soils, making a remarkable display in August and September. In the colder areas of Britain and in Zone 5 of the USA the crowns may need winter protection of bracken or straw.

## Pileostegia (Hydrangeaceae)

An excellent evergreen climber particularly suited for shady north walls, *Pileostegia viburnoides* is not grown as widely as it deserves, possibly because it tends to be a slow grower. It clings by aerial roots to walls, or trees, and bears 4 to 6 in (10–15 cm) lanceolate, dark green, leathery leaves. The creamy-white flowers produced in panicles during September have prominent stamens and are attractive and showy.

Hardy in Britain and a Zone 7 plant in the USA, where it is commonly termed 'Tanglehead', it is a native of China and was introduced by E. H. Wilson (1876–1930) to the Arnold Arboretum (USA) in 1908. It first flowered in Britain in 1914. Propagated by cuttings of ripe or semi-ripe wood in sand in a propagating frame under glass. The genus is closely allied to *Schizophragma*.

## Piptanthus (Leguminosae)

A good, easily grown wall plant, *P. laburnifolius* is seldom long-lived and not completely hardy in Britain. Sometimes called the

126

'Evergreen Laburnum' because its flowers resemble those of laburnum, it is naturally evergreen but loses its leaves in most British winters. It does well against walls in the London area making about 12 ft (3.5 m) of fairly spreading growth. The dark green leaves are trifoliate, a background for the bright yellow, pea flowers about $1\frac{1}{2}$ in (4 cm) long held in erect racemes and produced in fair abundance in May.

A native of the Himalayas and introduced in 1821, it is probably a Zone 8 plant in the USA. Easily propagated by seed and like so many leguminous shrubs should be pot grown until planted out.

## *Polygonum* (Polygonaceae)

One *Polygonum*, a climber, qualifies for this book — the so-called 'Russian Vine', *P. baldschuanicum*. A native of S. Turkestan, it was discovered in 1883 in an area then known as Baldshuan, hence the rather cumbrous specific name. It was introduced to Britain in 1894 via the St Petersburg Botanic Garden.

Quite superb as rapid coverage for sheds or derelict trees it is not a plant for walls. When first planted it may require some form of support such as wire or lattice but once started will grow and twine upon itself making an inextricable mass of growth which, although deciduous, will cover and blur the ugliest structure. Panicles of small white flowers envelop the plant in late summer so that it becomes a lovely frothy white tangle. The speed of growth of its young shoots in spring is fantastic and fascinating as they reach out, swaying in the wind to catch and twine upon any small support.

Like many plants it does best on a good loam soil; in very dry situations it can become thin and weedy. Completely hardy in Britain and a Zone 5 plant in the USA, it is propagated by cuttings of the summer wood taken with a heel attached and set in compost under mist or in a close frame.

## *Prunus* (Rosaceae)

Cherries are often grown on walls and very fine, easily protected crops can be grown thereby, but the ornamental species of *Prunus* are seldom seen on walls nowdays. Two are particularly

127

suited as wall plants and indeed grow and flower better in this way than in the open.

The first of these, *P. glandulosa*, known earlier as *P. japonica* 'Flore Pleno', was a garden plant in China and Japan long before it was introduced into Britain around 1774. It can be forced into early flower under glass and has been, and still is, used in this way. As a wall shrub it should be trained to wires or supports and the blossomed shoots pruned back almost to the old wood immediately after flowering. The young shoots that then arise are trained in neatly to cover the available wall space. Two varieties are listed by nurserymen: 'Albiplena' with large, double white flowers, and 'Sinensis', double bright-pink. Both flower in May.

The other and perhaps better known wall *Prunus* is *P. triloba*, a native of China introduced to Britain by Robert Fortune in 1885. This flowers at the end of March or early in April and should be treated in the same manner as *P. glandulosa*, with the blossoming twigs pruned back as soon as the flowers fade. The young shoots that are then made blossom the following year. The flowers are large, $1\frac{1}{2}$ in (4 cm) across, tightly double and clear pink; like *P. glandulosa* the plant can be used for forcing. *Prunus* are hardy enough (Zone 5 in the USA) but these two are at their best on south walls where they get sufficient sun to ripen their flowering wood. They are often budded or grafted onto plum stocks, and this can give rise to suckers which must be promptly removed. A good loam soil is desirable and if this is slightly chalky so much the better.

## *Pueraria* (Leguminosae)

Climbing at least 15 ft (4.5 m) in a season, *P. lobata*, the 'Kudzu Vine', a native of China and Japan, has some virtue as a coverage plant, although its scapes of light purple pea-flowers are seldom produced in Britain.

Introduced to the USA early in the twentieth century it was widely planted in the south mainly for soil conservation and as food for cattle. Finding the climate to its liking it has positively rampaged, and in areas from the south up to as far as Washington covers and destroys trees, and unless arrested envelops sheds and buildings and loops itself around poles and over power lines. Americans would not admit it as a garden plant but the British climate reduces it to just a useful plant for coverage. The stems with their grey-green trifoliate leaves will be cut back by frost and it only survives as a plant in the warmer areas, but if raised from seed and planted out when frost is past will produce rapid and satisfactory cover. The generic name honours a Danish Professor, M. N. Puerari (1765–1845).

## *Punica* (Punicaceae)

An orchard of pomegranates was possessed by King Solomon; the Children of Israel in the wilderness recalled the pomegranates they had enjoyed in Egypt; the prophet Muhammad said, 'eat the pomegranate for it purges the system of envy and hatred'. From all this it will be seen that the pomegranate, *Punica granatum*, is a plant with a long history linked to the Middle East; indeed it is reckoned to be indigenous to Iran and the neighbouring countries, and by the sixteenth century had been introduced into Britain. In 1548 it was grown in the garden of the Duke of Somerset at Syon Park and in 1629 Parkinson the London herbalist in his *Paradisi in Sole Paradisus Terrestris* advised that it be planted against walls.

The plant needs high temperatures and a dry atmosphere to produce fruit so in Britain it is of interest to gardeners only as an ornamental. A deciduous shrub, it has fresh green, shiny, elliptic 2 to 3 in (5–7.5 cm) long leaves, coppery-coloured when young and turning soft yellow in autumn. From July to September it bears highly decorative 1 to $1\frac{1}{2}$ in (2.5–4 cm) funnel-shaped, slightly fleshy, orange-red flowers. It needs a warm wall and a south-facing situation, a Zone 8 plant in the USA. There is a double form, 'Flore-Pleno', and records exist of striped and coloured variations: 'Albescens', creamy-white, 'Albo-Pleno', double creamy-white and 'Legrellii', striped red and yellowish-white. These, with the exception of 'Flore-Pleno', are not available in this country but may well exist in countries where the plant is grown commercially for its fruit. A dwarf form, *P. granatum* 'Nana', is free-flowering, slightly hardier and a very suitable south wall shrub for a patio garden. Propagated by seed or by cuttings taken in summer and inserted in sand in gentle heat.

## *Pyracantha* (Rosaceae)

The Firethorns or Pyracanths (from the Greek *pyr*, 'fire', and *akantha*, 'a thorn', a reference to the striking red berries) are shrubs perfectly hardy in Britain (Zone 6 or 7 in USA), but frequently grown as wall plants. In this situation they can be trained and clipped to make very attractive wall cover. They are fairly stiff and woody so cannot be moved away from walls like climbers and are best suited to walls that do not require the maintenance of painting etc. If it is necessary to use them against walls that require regular painting, selected shoots should be trained horizontally and/or perpendicularly on wires fixed at least 6 in (15 cm) away from the wall. These shoots will make woody stems or rods whose side shoots are clipped back annually to about 6 in (15 cm) either side of the rod. These shortened side shoots bear flowers and berries and because of the restricted width and their distance from the wall it is possible to paint behind them. This use of *Pyracantha* looks very effective on rather formal houses or houses in a modern style. The clipping back, best done after flowering, is also necessary for those conventionally planted against walls, unless there is a wide border and passage close to the wall is not necessary.

Pyracanths in Britain are generally evergreen although very severe winters may result in some leaf drop. They are not fastidious as to soil and do well on chalk, but as they will be long-lived residents generous border preparation before planting is desirable. *P. coccinea* from southern Europe and the near East has been grown in Britain since 1629 and is now represented in most gardens by the cultivar 'Lalandii', raised in France in 1874. Attention should be given, however, to the cultivars raised recently in the USA, Holland and Germany which have, in addition to larger, brighter berries, resistance to scab (*Fusicladium pyracanthi*), a fungal trouble which shows as black or grey scabbing on the berry, spoiling the colour and sometimes causing leaf drop and shoot dieback. These new varieties, mostly from crosses between *P. coccinea* and the Chinese *P. rogersiana* and *P. koidzumii*, are becoming available in the nursery trade. Among the best are 'Mohave' (**38**) with large orange-red berries, 'Telstar' with smaller dark-crimson berries; 'Orange Glow', large

130

orange-red berries from mid-September (later than 'Mohave'); 'Golden Glow', orange-yellow; and 'Orange Charmer', orange-red and very vigorous.

The Pyracanths are 'bonus plants' bearing as they do masses of showy white flowers in June followed of course by their main attraction, their berries, from August onwards; birds unfortunately have a liking for these but vary considerably, probably according to surroundings, in the toll they take. All Pyracanths are liable to attack by Fireblight (*Erwinia amylovora*). In Britain this bacterial disease is notifiable and if you see the characteristic, brown, singed dieback of leaves and young shoots, usually soon after flowering, you should inform the nearest office of the Ministry of Agriculture, who will give advice, based usually on careful selective pruning, on the control of the disease.

## *Rhaphiolepis* (Rosaceae)

More generally known as *Raphiolepis*, but here I have followed Bean (*Trees and Shrubs Hardy in the British Isles*, Vol. I, 8th edition, Murray 1970) in adopting the newer and presumably correct spelling. These are evergreen slow-growing shrubs needing the shelter of a south wall but possibly hardier than generally supposed.

The hybrid *R. x delacourii* is the best known and makes a rounded bush some 6 ft (1.8 m) high. It bears in spring and through to summer erect panicles of rosy-pink slightly fragrant flowers. A cross between the following two species, it was raised by M Delacour, gardener at the Villa Allerton, Cannes, in the late 1890s. 'Coates Crimson' is a good darker form.

*R. indica*, a native of China, with white flowers and pink stamens, is less hardy than the other parent of *R. x delacourii, R. umbellata*, whose white flowers, almost $\frac{3}{4}$ in (1.5 cm) across, are fragrant. A native of Japan and Korea, it was introduced to Britain about 1862. *Rhaphiolepis* can be propagated by seed or by cuttings of half-ripened wood taken in summer and inserted in sand frames with gentle bottom heat. They do not transplant well and so should be pot grown initially. I assume them to be Zone 7 plants in the USA.

CLIMBERS AND WALL PLANTS

## Ribes (Saxifragaceae)

One species of *Ribes* may be considered as a wall plant. *R. speciosum*, the Fuschia-flowered Gooseberry, although hardy, presents its red, long-stamened, pendulous flowers more attractively if trained to a wall than in the open. Flowering in April and May it benefits from a 'fruit grower's approach', in other words training and pruning as for gooseberries. To begin with, shoots should be tied in to the support wires and trained so as to cover the wall space available. This framework of branches is then annually spur pruned, that is the summer growth cut back in autumn to about 4 or 5 in (10–12 cm) and inward and soft unripened shoots removed. If bullfinches are a local fruit-bud pest, pruning is best left as late as possible, even up to January, lest by opening up the shrub one assists their depredations. A spiny shrub, it is not easily propagated by cuttings and is best layered. Introduced from California in 1828 by Mr Collie the Naval Surgeon on, appropriately enough, HMS *Blossom*; as a Californian native it is unlikely to thrive in Zones below 9.

## Robinia hispida (Leguminosae) (39)

This excellent shrub, the 'Rose Acacia', is often assumed to be a pink wisteria; flowering at the same time of year, June, and having pea-shaped flowers and similar leaves, the assumption is understandable but of course wrong. *Robinia hispida* is a native of the south-eastern United States, hardy there in Zone 5 and completely hardy in Britain.

An early American introduction, known in Britain since 1758, it was illustrated in *Curtis's Botanical Magazine* (t.311) as long ago as 1795 where in the language of the age it is described as 'not disposed to grow very tall even in America, it is most prudent indeed to keep it humble to the height of four or five feet, and to plant it in a sheltered part of the garden as its branches are liable to be broken by high winds.' This advice is as useful today as it was 186 years ago and explains its inclusion here as a wall shrub. Its stems should be securely tied in to wires or wall ties; any outgrowths that cannot be tied in should be pruned back in late summer to some 5 or 6 nodes.

132

The specific name, *hispida*, refers to the fine bristles borne on the stems, less formidable armour than the spines of many of its compatriots. Light green pinnate leaves show off to advantage the trusses of comparatively large, 1 in (2.5 cm) soft pink pea flowers. Propagated by seed or by grafting upon *Robinia pseudacacia* it does well in a dry situation and will accommodate a lime soil, additional points in its favour. An easily-grown decorative shrub that could be more widely planted as wall cover.

## *Rosa* (Rosaceae)

Mention climbing plants and people immediately think of roses followed perhaps by clematis or wisteria. Strictly speaking no rose is a climber; in nature they scramble by using their back-pointing thorns to lift themselves up through surrounding shrubs to the light and air. It is by artificial training and tying, however, that the rose can add to its many other virtues that of a climbing plant, and happily so for there can be few lovelier sights than a house wall covered with the sumptuous blooms of 'Madame Grégoire Staechelin' or the neat yellow rosettes of *Rosa banksiae* 'Lutea'. The long history of rose species and varieties is fascinating but outside the scope of this book, and the following brief descriptions of some of the best climbing roses and the purposes for which they are suited must suffice. If this spurs the reader to greater interest in climbing roses, he can satisfy this interest in full by perusal of the classic book *Climbing Roses Old and New* by Graham Thomas (Dent 1965).

### Roses for Walls
Walls make fine backgrounds for roses, particularly the larger flowered kinds. Most of the following are established favourites and well worth planting where conditions and wall height permit.

*R. x anemonoides* Vigorous, up to 15 ft (4.5 m) but needs a warm south wall. Single, clear shell-pink flowers produced from late May to late June. Slightly scented and floriferous; the cultivar 'Ramona' is a deep pink sport equally good.

133

'ALBERTINE' One of the best known climbing roses, and deservedly so. Satiny, coppery-pink full double flowers. Richly fragrant but gives only one tremendous burst of flower in mid-June. It will attain 18 ft (5.4 m) on a wall. Prune out flowered wood after flowering and tie in young shoots.

*R. banksiae* 'LUTEA' The Yellow Banksian Rose, a vigorous rose which will reach 30 ft (9.1 m) in favourable conditions. Best on a south-facing wall, slow-growing but superb when covered with its small, double, butter yellow slightly scented flowers. A plant of Chinese gardens, it was introduced by J. D. Parks in 1824 via the Calcutta Botanic Garden. Pruning should consist of removing only very old worn out wood. Flowers are produced on second and third year side shoots.

'BELLE PORTUGAISE' Derived from the rather tender *R. gigantea* this needs a south wall on which it will grow to 20 ft (6 m). A rose whose drooping leaves and creamy-salmon, loosely doubled, tea-scented flowers seem to convey the atmosphere of a sunny Edwardian rose garden.

*R. chinensis* 'MUTABILIS' A beautiful single rose whose flowers open a coppery buff, changing gradually to pink and ageing to pale crimson. During its flowering period in mid-June all these colours will be present, and this combined with the delicacy of the flowers gives a lovely effect. Not a strong grower, it appreciates a warm situation where its wood can ripen. It should be grown, more often than it is, as a wall rose, with the young wood tied in and occasional removal of old worn out wood in older plants. Grown on walls in this way it has achieved as much as 20 ft (6 m), but usually is little more than 8 ft (2.4 m). It is a very old rose and is sometimes sold under the name 'Tipo Ideale'.

'CLIMBING MADAME CAROLINE TESTOUT' The climbing form of the bush rose distributed in 1890 by that great French raiser M Pernet-Ducher of Venissieux near Lyons. The rose was selected by a London dressmaker, Mme Testout, who purchased the variety as part of a publicity campaign. The naming of roses in this way, now a commercial feature, is thus not new. Pernet-Ducher considered the pink seedling mediocre but the little dressmaker's judgement was more accurate, and 90 years later the variety with its prolific display of clear silver-pink, slightly

134

fragrant flowers against mid-green leaves is still highly regarded.

'CLIMBING CECILE BRUNNER' (**40**)   Vigorous, up to 20 ft (6 m). Flowers small, perfectly formed miniatures, double, pale blush pink borne in sprays. A lovely climber also suitable for training into trees.

'CLIMBING CRIMSON GLORY'   Climbing form of a one-time favourite bedding rose, superb fragrance and deep crimson flowers. Grows to about 6 ft (1.8 m) and a good rose for a north wall.

'CLIMBING ETOILE DE HOLLANDE'   Very often the climbing forms of hybrid tea varieties are still grown when the bush forms have been superseded by other varieties. Why this is so I am not sure, but climbing 'sports' are by the nature of things more vigorous, and it may be that the bush forms lose vigour over the years. Whatever the reason the deep velvety-crimson, strongly-scented flowers of this variety make it one of the best where a rose growing to about 6 ft (1.8 m) and at its best on a south wall is required.

'CLIMBING SHOT SILK'   One of the roses that do well in the typical British wet summer or indeed in an area subject to rain. Will achieve about 10 ft (3 m) on wall or pillar, profuse with its orange-salmon, deliciously-scented flowers.

'COCKTAIL'   A fairly modern rose (1957) that needs the shelter of a south wall. Single, bright crimson flowers with a large white centre, free-flowering with slight scent, very striking.

'GLOIRE DE DIJON'   A lovely old rose, first introduced in 1853. Buff-orange, double flowers 4 in (10 cm) across, strongly scented, flowering in early June and moderately recurrent. A good wall rose, the best of its colour.

'GUINEE'   Lovely dark, almost black red, fragrant flowers. Superb against white walls. Fairly vigorous up to about 12 ft (3.5 m), flowering from mid-June for three or four weeks. Inclined to become bare at the base.

'HELEN KNIGHT' (**41**)   Flowering in early May this rose has the advantage that our appreciative senses have not been numbed by the June plethora of lovely roses; even so few June roses have such a deep colour as this beauty, 2 in (5 cm) diameter, single golden yellow flowers backed by soft-green foliage but, alas, little scent. Flowering at the same time as the purple-pink *Clematis montana* 'Tetrarose', the two make a superb picture together. The name honours the memory of the wife of Frank Knight, Director of the Royal Horticultural Society's Garden from 1955 until 1969, who in 1964 obtained fertile seed from the cross of *R. ecae* with *R. pimpinellifolia* var. *altaica* and so raised this excellent plant. *Rosa ecae* was introduced from Afghanistan in 1880 by Dr Aitchison when making a survey of the Kurrum valley and the name is an adaptation of his wife's initials E.C.A. The other parent, a native of Siberia, is the larger form of what is often termed the Scotch rose. Inheriting from *R. ecae* a liking for sun, it is a plant for a south or west wall. No pruning other than that involved in training and tying is required.

'LAWRENCE JOHNSTONE' A seedling raised by the French firm Pernet-Ducher in 1923, the virtue of this fine rose was over-looked until the late Major Lawrence Johnstone saw it and brought the only plant to his garden at Hidcote. Here it remained relatively unsung until the Rosearian Graham Thomas saw it and asked if he could exhibit it before the Royal Horticultural Society where it received an Award of Merit and was subsequently named after the great gardener who introduced it. It is a splendid wall climber, semi-double, bright clear yellow, strongly-scented flowers with glossy green foliage, June-flowering.

'MADAME ALFRED CARRIERE' Vigorous, the flowers large, double, opening light cream and fading to white, floriferous and strongly-scented, light green leaves. A good wall rose that benefits from careful pruning, cutting out older flowering wood and carefully tying in the young shoots.

'MADAME GREGOIRE STAECHELIN' Sometimes called 'Spanish Beauty'. Vigorous and free-flowering up to some 20 ft (6.5 m). Large 5 in (12 cm) clear pink, scented flowers, commencing usually during the first week in June and giving a superb display for about three weeks.

'MAIGOLD' As the name suggests, May-flowering, and with large, semi-double, bronze-yellow flowers reddish in bud. Very fragrant it will grow up to 12 ft (3.5 m) with rich glossy foliage, a fine early-flowering rose with recurrent blossom.

'MERMAID' Dark glossy foliage and in Britain best on a sunny south or west wall. Large, single, canary-yellow flowers with a prominent boss of amber-coloured stamens. Shoots thorny and brittle and best trained and tied in when young, will grow up to 20 ft (6 m).

'NEW DAWN' A vigorous, comparatively large-flowered rambler up to 12 ft (3.5 m), which can do well trained on a north wall. Mid to late June, its pale blush silver-pink, scented flowers are freely produced against a background of glossy green foliage. Prune after flowering by cutting out old flowered wood and training in the young growth.

'PAUL'S SCARLET CLIMBER' A fine widely-grown rose that looks its best on a white or neutral wall, the slightly bluish red can clash with red-brick. Flowers in small clusters, slight scent, mid to late June.

### Roses for Pergolas, Catenaries, and Trees

The following can be, and sometimes are, planted against walls but their rambling style of growth makes them far more suitable for training onto pergolas or up into dead or outworn trees. Some are very suitable for training along lengths of rope or chain strung from post to post in line, the garden feature termed a catenary. They may be trained into trees or into robust evergreens such as holly against whose dark green leaves a white rose can look extremely effective.

'ALBERIC BARBIER' Buds of cream-white with a pale yolk-yellow centre, the open flowers white, double and with slight scent. Mid to late June, good glossy-green healthy foliage. A fine rose for fences or trees.

'AMERICAN PILLAR' The well-known rambler bearing clusters of single, bright pink, white-eyed single flowers. Should be hard pruned, flowered shoots being cut out and young growth trained in. Good for pergolas and fences even if somewhat overplanted.

'COMPLICATA' (42) Often termed (and quite rightly) a shrub rose, this lovely plant has such vigour that its growths will readily climb into a tree support as may be seen in plate 42. The flowers are large, single, a good clear pink with a white centre and with a

137

fine boss of yellow stamens. Very floriferous, rather like a large and very fine dog rose. A splendid rose where space and a compliant tree are available and, for those of us so limited, it does well on light sandy soils.

'CRIMSON SHOWER' Vigorous with light green glossy foliage, the small, crimson, double-rosette flowers borne in large trusses. A reliable rambler rose for pergola or fence.

'DOROTHY PERKINS' A name that seems to epitomise the rambler rose. Introduced in 1901 by Messrs Jackson & Perkins of Newark, New York, USA, and named after the grand-daughter of the then head of the company, Mr C. H. Perkins. Miss Dorothy Perkins became Mrs E. P. Estabrooke and resided at Germantown, Pennsylvania but her maiden name lives on in what is still a fine rose, although it is prone to mildew in a confined situation such as against a wall or fence. Trained into a tree it can be virtually mildew-free with its pink flowers showing to advantage against other leafage. It flowers from late June to mid-July and has little scent. It seems to typify the Edwardian era and indeed has been attractively planted in the rose garden of Polesden Lacey in Surrey, a National Trust property redolent of the Edwardian period.

*R. filipes* 'KIFTSGATE' The tree climbing rose par excellence. Capable of throwing a gorgeous mantle of great corymbs of single white, scented flowers over a dead or unwanted tree. Extremely vigorous it is a little slow to start but when established can throw shoots 20 ft long. The species was introduced from western China in 1908 but this form, 'Kiftsgate', named after the celebrated Oxfordshire garden, came to light in 1938. The July flowers are followed by a fine display of orange-red hips.

'FRANCIS E. LESTER' A fine rose to sprawl over a derelict stump, a hedgerow, or over a small tree. A vigorous rambler introduced in 1946, it bears bunches of cream white flowers, pink in bud and superbly fragrant, with good glossy green foliage.

'FRANÇOISE JURANVILLE' Vigorous with long shoots that enable it to achieve 20 ft (6 m) in trees. Full double rather flat, salmon-coral pink, scented flowers. Mid-June to July, excellent pergola or tree rose.

138

*R. longicuspis* Possibly not as well known nor as frequently planted as 'Kiftsgate', this rose is slightly less vigorous but establishes itself more quickly. Like 'Kiftsgate' it flowers in July and with a wealth of small white flowers each with a good centre of yellow stamens. In my opinion more fragrant than 'Kiftsgate' and with a scent reminiscent of oranges and bananas.

'SANDER'S WHITE RAMBLER' The best white in this class, vigorous with glossy foliage and fragrant flowers from mid-May to early July.

'VIOLETTE' Clusters of typically 'rambler' type, loosely double, purple-mauve flowers. Late June and excellent for a north-facing situation where the flowers more readily retain their mauve colour.

'WEDDING DAY' A vigorous, thorny seedling of *R. sinowilsonii*. Rich green foliage and clusters of creamy-white flowers with orange stamens and wonderful scent. A fine 'tree' rose which will also cover buildings or walls. Raised by the late Col. F. C. Stern and named because it opened its flowers on the anniversary of his wedding, 26th June.

**Roses for Pillars**
These are roses particularly suitable for training against pillars or the supports of a pergola since they rarely achieve more than 8 ft (2.4 m) in height. They are of course equally suitable for planting against walls where height is limited. Most are climbing forms of bush roses. The selection is wide, and the following are just a few.

'BANTRY BAY' Profuse flowering, light rose-pink, can attain 9 or 10 ft (3 m).

'CHAPLIN'S PINK CLIMBER' Vigorous up to 10 ft (3 m), glossy dark green foliage, semi-double bright pink. Suitable to train up and on to a pergola, also a good fence rose.

'CLIMBING MRS SAM MCGREDY' Deep coppery salmon-red, free-flowering, a large, lightly-scented rose.

'CLIMBING MADAME ABEL CHATENAY' A beautiful rose of light pink, a shade deeper in the centre, delicious scent.

139

'CLIMBING ALLGOLD' Slightly scented, bright and unfading yellow semi-double flowers; should be pruned lightly.

'COPENHAGEN' A good large, fragrant double scarlet, apt to become leggy at the base.

'DANSE DU FEU' Very free-flowering, bright scarlet crimson, semi-double and slightly scented. Showy, vigorous and can be trained as a wall rose.

'EASLEA'S GOLDEN RAMBLER' Not a rambler, but since it will attain 12 ft (3.5 m) or 15 ft (4.5 m) it is excellent for planting against a pillar and extending over and along a pergola or catenary. Large full, butter-yellow flowers, lovely scent and glossy green foliage.

'GOLDEN SHOWERS' (43) An upright grower, large double flowers opening golden yellow but becoming paler as they age. Fragrant and flowering over a long period.

'HANDEL' A lovely cream-coloured flower heavily edged pink, particularly good as a pillar rose.

'PAUL'S LEMON PILLAR' Indeed a pillar rose since the flowers tend to droop and one is thus able to look up into them. Strongly-scented, double creamy-lemon.

'SCHOOLGIRL' (44) Vigorous and apt to get leggy, lightly-scented, soft apricot-orange full flowers.

**Roses for Fences**
The roses listed as suited for pillars and some of those for walls are equally suitable for growing against fences. These may be wattle hurdles, interwoven wood strip, close board or ranch type fencing. They need generally to be at least 5 ft in height although it is possible to train the rambling, almost creeping wichuriana type such as 'Alberic Barbier' or 'Françoise Juranville' along the top rail of low fences. These and some of the less vigorous ramblers such as 'Sander's White Rambler' and 'Crimson Shower' as well as 'New Dawn', 'Paul's Scarlet Climber' and 'Gloire de Dijon' are equally useful for fence coverage.

If you have that abomination, chain-link fencing (beloved of government establishments and local authorities), consider the advice given on p. 22. Plant ivy, good-natured uncomplaining

140

ivy, green or variegated that will give evergreen cover. Keep it clipped once a year and plant ramblers against it. 'Sander's White Rambler', 'Crimson Shower', 'American Pillar' — any or all will give colour and delight, and if pruned (as they must be) annually after flowering will present a neat tight, pleasant fence.

### Roses for Patio Walls

There are two roses that I am inclined to term 'patio roses'. They are completely thornless and in my opinion eminently suitable for areas where people may be in contact with plants and where thorn-bearing plants may not be welcome. They are also of course so very suitable for gardens designed specifically for blind people. The two comprise that delightful old rose 'Zéphirine Drouhin', raised in 1868, bright cerise, semi-double, lightly scented, mid to late June and moderately recurrent, and its lovely shell-pink sport 'Kathleen Harrop'. Suitable for clothing low walls surrounding patios they will flower happily on a north-facing situation.

## *Rubus* (Rosaceae)

The genus *Rubus* containing the invaluable blackberry, prickly target of so many late-summer family expeditions, raspberry and loganberry offers perhaps more to the kitchen than to the flower garden, and although scores of the 400 or so known species are scrambling or climbing plants only a few deserve recognition here.

One of these is *R. cissoides* var. *pauperatus*, the 'Pauper's Berry' so called from its almost leafless denuded state. It is sometimes listed as *R. squarrosus* and sometimes as a variety of *R. australis*. A scrambling, zigzagging climber in which the leaves are reduced to little more than a prickly mid-rib, it is armed with tiny white prickles and bears narrow-petalled, yellowish-white flowers; a plant of no beauty but of singular interest it is a native of New Zealand and its date of introduction to Britain uncertain. Being rather tender it requires wall shelter in most of Britain and is a Zone 8 plant in the USA. In contrast the following are completely hardy, Zone 3 in the USA.

*Rubus laciniatus*, the 'Fern-leaved' or 'Cut-leaved Bramble' is a variation of our common blackberry. The leaves are elegant and it fruits perfectly well but is heavily thorned. Far better to grow the thornless form widely sold as the 'Thornless Blackberry', useful and attractive if trained on a fence or pergola.

*Rubus ulmifolius* 'Bellidiflorus' is a form of another of our native blackberries. It has completely double flowers like neat pink rosettes borne profusely in panicles from July until autumn. Very vigorous, prickly and growing well in deep shade it is a plant for the wild garden and can look very effective scrambling up a dark green prickly holly — a case of Greek meeting Greek as regards thorns!

## *Salvia* (Labiatae)

Several kinds of sage make pleasing low shrubs if planted against a south wall. This of course is true also of the well known kitchen herb, *Salvia officinalis*, which in its various coloured leaved varieties thrives in such a situation, but will grow equally well elsewhere. The following are attractive sages grown for flower rather than leaf and needing wall shelter, given that they can be extremely decorative, flowering from July until autumn.

Capable of making a shrub up to 4 ft (1.2 m) high, *S. grahamii* has rather oval round-toothed leaves and bears bright scarlet flowers in racemes up to 1 ft (30 cm) long. The leaves when crushed smell of blackcurrant. It takes its name from a Mr. J. G. Graham who discovered it in Mexico in 1830.

Like *S. grahamii*, *S. greggii* has square stems but leaves oblong and of dull pale green and only faintly smelling of blackcurrant. It will make a shrub about 3 ft (90 cm) high, bearing flowers of carmine-red. Discovered by a Dr Gregg in 1848 in Mexico.

In favourable situations *S. neurepia* will attain 6 ft or 7 ft (1.8–2 m). The leaves are ovate, light-green, softly hairy and strongly aromatic. It is a native of Mexico, and the flowers in long racemes are scarlet-magenta.

The 'Pineapple Sage', *S. rutilans*, is worth growing if only for the unusual scent of its ovate, downy leaves when crushed. In addition it has the merit of magenta-crimson flowers freely produced.

A strong grower, *S. involucrata* var. 'Bethellii' has ovate to heart-shaped leaves and bright rosy-crimson flowers that are sticky to the touch.

All these sages, Zone 9 plants in the USA, can be short-lived, but are readily propagated by soft summer cuttings inserted in sand in a heated frame.

## *Schisandra* (Schisandraceae)

Twining climbers for shade or semi-shade, suited for walls or for growing over fences or trees, liking a cool root-run but amenable to chalk. Reasonably hardy in Britain the *Schisandra* is the 'Himalayan Magnolia Vine' of the USA where it is a Zone 8 plant. The small fleshy flowers in shades of red to white are solitary, from $\frac{1}{2}$ to 1 in (1.2–2.5 cm) across and usually borne on quite long, pendulous stalks. The plant is dioecious, that is individual plants bear flowers of one sex only; in order therefore to obtain the quite attractive scarlet berries, plants of both sexes are required. These can be planted close together so as to climb up the chosen support as one. The following species, all deciduous, are likely to be available from specialist nurserymen.

*Schisandra chinensis*, a vigorous plant that can achieve up to 30 ft (9 m), the flowers are fragrant, white or pale pink and produced in April or May. Introduced from China in 1860, the dried wood is reputedly fragrant.

Introduced from China by Wilson in 1908, *S. rubrifolia* will climb to about 20 ft (6 m), the flowers a glowing deep crimson in late May, probably the best of those grown.

Climbing to 30 ft (9 m) the form of *S. propinqua* called 'Sinensis' is hardier than the type and bears yellowish-orange flowers in late summer, introduced from China in 1907.

*Schisandra sphenanthera* bears its orange-red flowers in May and June and may be recognised by its slightly warty shoots, it too came to use from China in 1907.

All the *Schisandras* can be propagated by seed or layers or by cuttings of half-ripened wood taken in July or August and inserted in sand in a warm frame.

## *Schizophragma* (Hydrangeaceae)

At a casual glance members of this genus look very much like the climbing *Hydrangea* (*see* page 88), but although closely related they differ markedly by having large single-petalled flowers at the edges of the flat plate-like inflorescence instead of the much less conspicuous four-petalled flowers of the *Hydrangea*.

Two species are in cultivation, *S. hydrangeoides*, a native of Japan introduced to Britain in 1879, has round-ovate coarsely-toothed leaves and flower bracts of whitish yellow. A form with pink to red bracts received an Award of Merit from the Royal Horticultural Society in 1939. The other species, *S. integrifolium*, has similar leaves but more finely toothed, larger flower heads and bracts that may be as much as $2\frac{1}{2}$ to $3\frac{1}{2}$ in (6–9 cm) long. Both flower in July and both may be propagated by summer cuttings inserted in a sand frame. Zone 5 plants in the USA, both species are suitable for north- or east-facing walls and will attain 30 to 40 ft (9 to 12 m) in time. Of these and *Hydrangea petiolaris* (*see* page 88), *S. integrifolium* is the most decorative and probably the best garden plant.

## *Senecio* (Compositae)

Three species of this vast genus are of interest as wall plants or climbers. The hardiest and most widely grown is the shrubby, evergreen, grey-leaved plant usually known as *Senecio laxifolius* or *S. greyi*. In fact neither name is correct, for botanical detective work by Charles Jefferey at the Kew Herbarium has shown the plant to be a hybrid, probably of crosses and back-crosses between *Senecio laxifolius*, *S. greyi* and *S. compactus*. It was first distributed from Dunedin Botanic Garden, Otago, New Zealand about 1910, and Mr Jefferey took the suggestion of Roy Lancaster, formerly Curator of the Hillier Arboretum, and published the name *Senecio* (Dunedin Hybrid) 'Sunshine'. The name perfectly describes this superb garden plant which is completely hardy and does not require wall protection. Another virtue and indeed the only reason for its inclusion here is that of being an admirable plant to give coverage to the bare lower stems of climbers. The grey foliage topped in July with masses of yellow daisy flowers can make a grand foil to clematis in their various shades of blue, or to roses from dark reds to white. After flowering the flowered shoots should be pruned back; young growth that will flower the following year will rapidly appear and the bush in this way is prevented from becoming leggy.

The second species, *S. monroi*, has leaves slightly more green than grey and wavy at the edges. It is of interest but is less good as a garden plant. Like *S.* 'Sunshine' it can be propagated by cuttings of semi-ripe wood set in sand and peat in a cold frame in late summer. Both are natives of New Zealand and probably Zone 6 plants in the USA.

The third species, *S. scandens*, is rarely seen in gardens, yet once happy and established it bears masses of yellow daisy flowers in late summer and autumn when flowers are scarce and can contrast superbly with the late flowers one often gets on clematis such as 'Gypsy Queen' or 'Jackmanii Superba'. A native of China and Japan it may be hardier than people think, indeed the late Margery Fish recorded that it sowed itself in her Somerset garden and its praises have been sung from gardens in Suffolk and the West of Scotland. It is an evergreen and will climb, scramble perhaps is the better word, up to 15 ft (4.5 m); it has ovate to triangular bright green leaves and may be propagated by seed or by soft summer cuttings taken in late summer and inserted in sand in gentle heat. Probably a Zone 8 plant in the USA.

## *Solanum* (Solanaceae)

'Not planted as widely as it deserves' is almost a garden book cliché — be that as it may, this phrase is very true of the two *Solanums* considered as wall plants, particularly the hardier of the two, *S. crispum*. Vigorous, semi-evergreen, lime-loving, it is a sub-shrub that will extend its herbaceous stems 12 ft (3.5 m) in a season, bearing corymbs of blue-purple flowers similar individually to the flowers of the potato to whose family it belongs. The selected clone 'Glasnevin', sometimes called 'Autumnalis' is hardier and superbly floriferous. The main display, a billowing mass of blue on a well-grown plant comes in July, but flowers continue into September. A native of Chile, it was introduced to Britain in 1830.

145

The other species, *S. jasminoides*, is a fast-growing, semi-evergreen climber with twining stems and profusely borne clusters of pale blue flowers. It is less hardy than *S. crispum* and requires in Britain a south or west wall; both species are Zone 8 plants in the USA. The white form 'Album' is the more frequently grown, and deservedly so, for it is a particularly clear and lovely white enhanced by the central boss of yellow stamens. A native of Brazil, it has been in British gardens since 1838. Both species can be propagated by summer cuttings inserted in a close frame.

## *Teucrium* (Labiatae) (45)

The Shrubby Germander, *T. fruticans*, can be trained as a pleasant little wall plant for a sunny situation, indeed it will not survive without such protection. It makes a slow-growing shrub 2 to 5 ft (50–150 cm) high, its criss-crossing square stems bearing evergreen ovate leaves; both stems and the leaf undersides are white felted and make a pleasing background for the blue flowers. These are interesting in having a comparatively deep and wide lip, making the flower look like a little blue face with a long and large chin. The foliage is fragrant when crushed or handled. A native of Spain, it was introduced to Britain in 1714 by the then Duchess of Beaufort. Propagated by cuttings of young growth set in sand in a propagating frame during summer. In the USA it is a Zone 7 plant with protection.

## *Thladiantha* (Cucurbitaceae)

There seems some dispute as to the origin of this rather curious generic name. Nicholson's *Dictionary of Gardening* (1885) gives it as the Greek *thladias*, 'compressed', and *anthe*, 'a flower', 'owing it is said to the plant being first described from a pressed specimen'. The *RHS Dictionary of Gardening* (1951), however, has it from the Greek *thladias*, 'a eunuch', and *anthos*, 'flower', because 'Flowers on the type specimen of *T. dubia* had the anthers suppressed as if castrated.' Perhaps Nicholson was persuaded by the ethics of the Victorian era!

146

Introduced from China to the Paris Jardin des Plantes in 1861 *T. dubia* is a herbaceous tendril climber rather like a cucumber plant with numerous golden-yellow cucumber type flowers. It is dioecious, that is male and female flowers are on separate plants. The male plant is the more decorative and floriferous and indeed is the only form I have seen. Suprisingly for a Cucurbit it is hardy in Britain, probably Zone 7 in the USA, and on a south or west wall makes a very fine display. It will top an 8 ft (2.5 m) wall, but leaves and flowers thin out somewhat at the base and it is a good plan to front it with screen plants (*Caryopteris* maybe, whose blue flowers would coincide with the July–September flowering of this very rarely seen climber).

## *Trachelospermum* (Apocynaceae)

Climbers for sunny sheltered walls, self-clinging, evergreen, producing dense leafage and sweet-scented creamy-white flowers.

Two species are suitable for planting in Britain. The most commonly seen, *T. jasminoides*, is in fact the less hardy of the two. Rather slow-growing it will in time achieve a height of 20 ft (6 m) in mild areas. The leathery, oval-lanceolate leaves are dark shining green, the flowers about 1 in (2 cm) wide, borne in terminal and axillary clusters, white and very fragrant. Introduced to Britain from China by Robert Fortune in 1844, it is a favoured climber in the southern USA, Zones 7 and 8, where it will clamber from wall to roof making a thatch of stems that will accommodate birds' nests. Established plants flower well in Britain but severe winters can cut it back very badly. There is a variegated form that is not, to my mind, an improvement.

The other species, *T. asiaticum*, is similar but hardier and more compact in growth, the flowers a little smaller and in age inclining more to a buff yellow colour, but equally fragrant. It is a native of Korea and Japan. *Trachelospermums* prefer a slightly acid soil, and the addition of peat at planting time is a good practice. All exude a milky juice when the stems are cut and may be propagated by cuttings of half-ripened wood in gentle heat in sand/peat composts in July and August.

147

## *Tripterygium* (Celastraceae)

Scandent climbing shrubs best planted to clamber into small trees. The leaves, ovate or elliptic, are between 2 and 6 in (5–15 cm) long. The flowers, borne in late summer, are small, greenish-white and followed by clusters of attractive pale green winged fruits.

*Tripterygium regelii* from Japan was introduced in 1905, will attain some 18 ft (6 m) and is perfectly hardy, Zone 4 in the USA. The other species, *T. wilfordii*, once known as *forrestii*, is less hardy, Zone 7 in the USA, but more vigorous, being capable of 40 ft (12 m). Although it will grow in most areas with wall protection, its vigour rules it out as a wall plant, but it is very suitable for trees in mild areas. The inflorescence is large, up to 1 foot (30 cm) long and the winged fruits reddish in colour. A native of southern China, Formosa and Burma, it was introduced by George Forrest (1873–1932) in 1913. Both species may be propagated by seeds or quite easily by layering the long trailing growths.

## *Tropaeolum* (Tropaeolaceae)

This genus contains the well-known annual nasturtium as well as several perennial climbers that make annual growth which dies back to underground tubers or rhizomes. Foremost of these and the only hardy one is *T. speciosum* (**46**), a plant whose crimson-scarlet, nasturtium-like flowers make a delightful picture when scrambling through evergreens such as camellias, rhododendrons or yew hedging and flowering from July to September. Its popular name, 'Scotch Flame Flower', gives a clue to its successful cultivation for the cool, moist summers of Scotland suit it admirably, duplicating the conditions of its native Chile whence it was introduced in 1846.

The fleshy rhizomes should be planted about 9 in (22 cm) deep in good soil, sufficiently far from the intended host shrub to avoid its hungry roots, the soil should be always moist and free of lime. With similar treatment it is a lovely climber for a north wall, suitable lattice or wire being needed for the twining leaf-stalks to embrace.

Another *Tropaeolum*, the tender annual *T. perigrinum*, some-

148

times called *T. canariensis*, is worth while sowing to climb up and mingle its small, feathered, yellow flowers with blue or purple clematis.

## *Vitis* (Vitaceae)

Few climbers can be of more historic importance than the vine, linked as it is to mankind's development in the western world. Although the genus is essentially valued for its nutritive and commercial importance it also contains some ornamental kinds grown for their leaf effects. The following, with the exception of the *V. vinifera* varieties, are best suited as climbers on trees or on very large structures.

### *V. amurensis*
Introduced from the Amur region of Manchuria around 1854. A vigorous hardy species with reddish shoots and fine autumn colour of crimson and purple. A Zone 2 plant.

### *V. coignetiae*
Widely planted and a superb vine where there is room for the 60 or 90 ft (18–27 m) height that it can attain on trees. The leaves, 4 to 8 in (10–20 cm) wide and sometimes larger, are russet in colour beneath and turn crimson and scarlet in autumn. A native of Japan, it was first introduced by the East Indian Merchant company of Jardine and Matheson to Waterer's Nursery at Knaphill, Surrey. Later in 1875 seeds were imported from Japan to France by a Madame Coignet from whom the plant takes its name. It is the 'Glory Vine Grape' of America where it is a Zone 5 plant.

### *V. davidii*
Easily recognised by the hooked spines on the stems. A vigorous luxuriant climber with fine autumn colour. Introduced from Central China in 1885. USA Zone 2.

### *V. riparia*
The very hardy (Zone 2) 'Riverbank Grape' of America. Worth growing for its mignonette scented flowers and shining green foliage, a vigorous high climber.

### *V. vinifera*
The grape of commerce of which several ornamental kinds are

149

well suited for pergolas and fences or for south-facing walls. Zone 6 plants in the USA.

'APIIFOLIA' The cut-leaved parsley vine.

'BRANDT' A popular hardy fruiting vine whose leaves turn dark red and purple. It was raised in Paris, Ontario, in the 1860s.

'INCANA' The 'Dusty Miller' grape. Leaves grey-green and covered with white cob-webbed down. Can look very fine growing up and through a purple-flowering plum (*Prunus cerasifera* 'Pissardii').

'PURPUREA' The reverse of the above, leaves a deep vinous purple, very effective if grown into the grey-leaved weeping pear (*Pyrus salicifolia* 'Pendula').

Vines on trees must inevitably be left to their own devices; those on pergolas should have the long new shoots shortened in summer and be pruned hard back like greenhouse vines in winter. They may be propagated by lengths of semi-ripe wood, 4 to 8 in (10–20 cm) taken in autumn and inserted in sand frames with a little bottom heat. *V. coignetiae* is, however, often raised from seed.

## *Wattakaka* (Asclepiadaceae)

A curious name for a seldom grown plant whose scented flowers are very like those of the greenhouse plant, *Hoya carnosa*. A deciduous twining shrub, one species, *W. sinensis*, can be grown in Britain with wall protection but is a Zone 8 plant in the USA. Formerly known as *Dregea sinensis*, it can reach 10 ft (3 m) on a warm sheltered wall. The leaves are ovate, grey felted beneath, the flowers white and waxy and with red dots, introduced from China in 1907. The first species discovered, *W. volubilis*, was found in India and the generic name is based on the Malabar native name of *Wattakaka-rodi*. Easily propagated by seed sown under glass.

## *Weigela* (Caprifoliaceae)

*Weigelas* are hardy shrubs (USA Zone 5) and not in need of wall protection, but it is worth while drawing attention to the attraction of one variety, *W. florida* 'Foliis Purpureis', when planted against whitened walls. The beauty of this shrub lies in its purple leaves enhanced by the soft pink-purple, foxglove-like flowers produced in June. A deciduous shrub, it can be trained and tied in to wires or nails and is very suited for north or east walls. An easily-grown plant in any soil, wood that has flowered should be pruned out, tying in the young growth to replace it. Easily propagated by autumn cuttings (*see* page 39). The parent species, *W. florida*, was introduced from China in 1845 by the plant collector Robert Fortune.

## *Wisteria* (Leguminosae)

In its period of flower the wisteria surpasses all climbers and pro-bably all hardy ornamentals for sheer display. On mature, well-grown specimens the flowers, each like a miniature sweet-pea, hang in racemes; a profusion of pale mauve, faintly-scented blossom that can be breathtaking. Native to China, Japan and the USA, the generic name honours Caspar Wistar (1761–1818), a professor at the University of Pennsylvania, and was bestowed on the genus, which was previously called *Glycine*, by the botan-ist Thomas Nuttall shortly after Wistar's death.

The first species introduced into Britain was *W. frutescens* in 1724. A native of the south-east USA, it is not so strong a grower as the other species nor does it produce so fine a display. It was the introduction from China in 1816 of *W. sinensis* (**48**) that made the western world aware of the plant's beauty and potential. Indeed as W. J. Bean, author of *Trees and Shrubs Hardy in the British Isles* (John Murray, 1st ed, 1914), wrote, 'no climber ever brought to this country has added more to the beauty of gardens'. Small wonder that soon after its introduction plants were sold for 6 guineas apiece, a sum nearer to £500 in today's currency.

*Wisteria sinensis* will reach 60 to 100 ft (18–30 m) on a tree and will comfortably clothe a two-storey house. The pinnate leaves have between 9 and 13 leaflets and the stems twine in an anti-clockwise direction. The fragrant mauve or deep lilac flowers each about 1 in (2.5 cm) long are carried in racemes 9 to 12 in (20–30 cm) long and appear in May before the leaves. The flowers open simultaneously on the truss making the plant's display more sensational, albeit briefer than that of *W. floribunda*, where they open from the 'shoulder' of the raceme in succession down to the tip. The plant is hardy enough but flowers better in the south of Britain. Late spring frosts can destroy the buds and thus wall-protected plants give more reliable displays. Several varieties are listed: 'Alba' is a slightly milky white, 'Black Dragon' has double dark-purple flowers and 'Plena' double lilac flowers. The latter two flower less freely. In the USA where wisterias are popular, *W. sinensis* is listed as a Zone 5 plant.

Of the remaining species known, only *W. floribunda* is generally available and grown. It was imported in 1830 by Philipp von Siebold from Japan into Belgium and thence to Britain. An equally lovely plant, its pinnate leaves have 13 to 19 leaflets and the stems, unlike those of *W. sinensis*, twine in a clockwise direction. The flowers fragrant and bluish purple are borne in slender racemes 6 to 10 in (13–25 cm) long. It flowers later, in June, and appears to be a little hardier, Zone 4 in the USA.

In 1874 came the introduction from Japan of a garden variety 'Macrobotrys', now called 'Multijuga', with flower racemes of great length; these are often 2 to 3 ft (60–90 cm) in Britain and reputedly over 4 ft (1.2 m) in Japan. For some years regarded as a distinct species, it is now established as a variety of *W. floribunda*; it has the same number of leaflets and twines in the same clockwise direction. It is superbly effective grown to cover a bridge, pergola or arch where the full beauty of the long hanging racemes can be appreciated. *W. sinensis* is the better plant for walls and buildings. Other varieties of *W. floribunda* are: 'Alba' (**47**), a fine plant with flowers that are truly white; 'Rosea', a lilac pink; 'Violacea', violet-blue; and 'Violacea Plena' double violet-blue. Variegated leaved forms of both *W. sinensis* and *W. floribunda* have been recorded but are of no merit at all.

Wisterias are not fastidious as to soil but a good loam is preferable. They are propagated by grafting or by seed but not all seedlings flower well or are of good colour. It is important therefore when buying to obtain the plants from a reliable nurseryman with an assurance that they are grafted plants. Such plants may cost more but the first cost is immaterial in a plant that can provide over the years such a wealth of bloom.

# Plants for Selected Sites

The question often arises, 'what can we grow on the north side of our house?' This is not always easy to answer, as much depends on the degree of exposure. A north wall in Aberdeen is not the same as a north wall in Aldershot! Soil, too, affects the choice vastly.

The following lists attempt to give some guidance, but naturally it will be necessary to refer to the plant descriptions to determine any particular requirements. It will be seen that the list of plants for south and west aspects is far longer than that for north and east. This is due to two factors; firstly, many plants that will grow on north walls are also well worth growing on south or west walls (*Senecio* 'Sunshine' is a good example); secondly, when you have south walls, it is as well to be adventurous and to try many of the lovely plants that can be grown. The note 'see list' implies that some varieties or species are suited but others not.

## North and East Walls and Aspects

*Aristolochia macrophylla*
*Asteranthera*
*Azara*
*Berberidopsis*
*Camellia* (see list)
*Caryopteris*
*Chaenomeles*
*Chimonanthus*
*Choisya*
*Clematis* (see list)
*Cotoneaster horizontalis*
*Euonymus radicans*
*Forsythia*
*Fuchsia*
*Garrya*
*Hedera* (see list)
*Hydrangea*
*Itea*
*Jasminum*

*Kerria*
*Lathyrus* (see list)
*Lonicera*
*Mitraria*
*Osmanthus*
*Paeonia*
*Parthenocissus*
*Periploca*
*Philadelphus* (see list)
*Philesia*
*Pileostegia*
*Pyracantha*
*Rosa* (see list)
*Schisandra*
*Schizophragma*
*Senecio* (see list)
*Tropaeolum speciosum*
*Weigela*

# South and West Walls and Aspects

*Abelia*
*Abeliophyllum*
*Abutilon*
*Acacia*
*Actinidia kolomikta*
*Araujia*
*Buddleia* (see list)
*Caesalpinia*
*Calceolaria*
*Callistemon*
*Campsis*
*Carpenteria*
*Caryopteris*
*Ceanothus*
*Cestrum*
*Chaenomeles*
*Chimonanthus*
*Choisya*
*Clematis* (see list)
*Clerodendrum*
*Clianthus*
*Cobaea*
*Colquhounia*
*Crinodendron*
*Cytisus battandieri*
*Decumaria*
*Dendromecon*
*Desfontainea*
*Eccremocarpus*
*Fatsia*
*Fendlera*
*Ficus*
*Fremontodendron*
*Fuchsia*
*Grevillea*
*Hoheria*

*Ipomoea*
*Jasminum nudiflorum*
*Kadsura*
*Kerria*
*Lagerstroemia*
*Lapageria*
*Lardizabala*
*Lathyrus pubescens*
*Leonotis*
*Leptospermum*
*Lippia citriodora*
*Mandevilla*
*Mimulus aurantiacus*
*Mutisia*
*Passiflora*
*Perovskia*
*Phlomis*
*Phygelius*
*Piptanthus*
*Prunus* (see list)
*Punica*
*Rhaphiolepis*
*Ribes speciosum*
*Robinia*
*Rosa* (see list)
*Rubus cissoides*
*Salvia*
*Senecio* (see list)
*Solanum*
*Teucrium*
*Thladiantha*
*Trachelospermum*
*Wattakaka*
*Weigela*
*Wisteria*

154

# Pergolas and Pillars

Clematis (see list)
Cobaea
Humulus (see list)

Rosa (see list)
Vitis (see list)
Wisteria

# Fences

Clematis (see list)
Hedera (see list)

Humulus (see list)
Rosa (see list)

# Sheds and Buildings

Akebia
Celastrus orbiculatus
Hedera (see list)
Jasminum officinale
Lonicera

Menispermum canadense
Parthenocissus (see list)
Periploca
Polygonum baldschuanicum
Pueraria lobata

# Patios and Low Walls

Abutilon megapotamicum
Ampelopsis brevipedunculata
'Elegans'
Aristolochia sempervirens
Eccremocarpus
Euonymus radicans
'Variegatus'
Hedera (see list)

Lippia citriodora
Mimulus aurantiacus

Perovskia
Teucrium

# Climbers for Small Trees

Ampelopsis (see list)
Berchemia giraldiana
Celastrus orbiculatus
Clematis (see list)
Hedera colchica 'Dentata

Variegata'
Holboellia coriacea
Lonicera
Menispermum canadense
Periploca

155

*Polygonum baldschuanicum*       *Tripterygium*
*Rosa* (see list)                *Vitis* (see list)
*Rubus ulmifolius*               *Wisteria*
'Bellidiflorus'

## Climbers for Tall Trees

*Actinidia* (see list)           *Vitis* (see list)
*Ampelopsis megalophylla*        *Wisteria*

# Glossary

This list is appended to avoid confusion or doubt as to the meaning of the few technical terms used in this book.

**Adventitious**  Roots arising from other parts of the plant than the seed. Usually implies roots on aerial stems.

**Axil**  The junction of leaf stalk to stem.

**Bottom heat**  A form of heating under a propagating frame usually supplied by electric cable buried in the sand.

**Budding**  Propagation by the insertion of a leaf-bud of one species or cultivar into a prepared cut in the stem of the stock, a rooted plant which will need to be a closely allied species.

**Calyx**  The outer part of the flower, the usually leafy sepals.

**Cordate**  Heart-shaped.

**Corolla**  The inner and normally decorative part of the flower, the petals.

**Corymb**  A flat topped or dome shaped flower-head where the outer flowers open first.

**Cultivar**  A garden variety of a plant, literally a 'cultivated variety'.

**Deciduous**  With leaves that seasonally fall, not persistent over the winter.

**Dioecious**  Male and female flowers each on separate plants.

**Elliptic**  Widest at the middle narrowing at each end.

**Evergreen**  Remaining green during winter.

**Genus**  A group of related species.

**Humus**  Well-rotted organic matter.

| | |
|---|---|
| **Labiate** | Flower structure like the Dead-nettle (*Lamium*); a zygomorphic flower with a prominent lip. |
| **Lanceolate** | Lance-shaped, widening above the base, tapering to the apex. |
| **Larval** | The caterpillar stage of many pests, the state of being a larva. |
| **Leaf-bud cuttings** | A leaf with a bud in its axil, taken with a small portion of stem and inserted as a cutting. |
| **Mist** | Name for a system of propagation where a fine water spray is misted over cuttings at regular intervals by automatic means. |
| **Monoecious** | Male and female flowers separate but appearing on the same plant. |
| **Monotypic** | A genus consisting of one species only. |
| **Mulch** | A surface dressing of compost, manure or in nature fallen and rotting leaves. |
| **Nodes** | The 'joints' in stems and branches, botanically, the point where leaf-stalks emerge from the stem. |
| **Ovate** | Where length is only just greater than breadth and broadest below the centre. |
| **Palmate** | Lobed or divided in hand-like fashion. |
| **Panicle** | A branching raceme. |
| **Peltate** | Umbrella-like; the leaf stalk in the centre. |
| **Perfoliate** | When a pair of opposite leaves fuse at their base so as to hug the stem. |
| **Pinnate** | With leaflets arranged on either side of a central mid-rib. |
| **Pupa** | The metamorphic stage between caterpiller or larva and moth, butterfly or fly. |
| **Raceme** | A simple elongated inflorescence with stalked flowers. |
| **Saprophytic** | Normally living on dead matter. |
| **Semi-evergreen** | Losing some or all leaves in severe weather. |
| **Sepal** | One of the segments of a calyx. |
| **Species** | A group of closely related interbreeding individuals. |

| Spent Hops | The residue from brewing operations, a good source of organic material when obtainable. |
| Spur | A short stiff branchlet. |
| Stamen | The male organ of a flower, comprising a stalk or filament and the anther containing the pollen. |
| Staminodes | Sterile stamens or organs resembling stamens. |
| Stigma | The receiving organ of the pollen, usually the summit of the pistil. |
| Stipules | Leafy appendages, usually 2, at the base of a leaf stalk. |
| Style | The middle part of the pistil. |

# Bibliography

Bean, W.J., *Trees and Shrubs Hardy in the British Isles*, 8th edition (revised), Murray 1980

Bush-Brown, L. and J., *America's Garden Book*, Scribner 1952

Coats, Alice M., *Garden Shrubs and their Histories*, Vista 1963

Fisk, Jim, *Clematis*, 2nd edition, Cassell/The Royal Horticultural Society 1985

Fisk, Jim, *Clematis: The Queen of Climbers*, Cassell, 1989

Hadfield, Miles, *A History of British Gardens*, Hamlyn 1969

Hadfield, Harling and Highton, *British Gardeners*, Zwemmer 1980

Lloyd, Christopher, *Clematis*, 2nd edition, Viking 1989

Pearce, S.A., *Climbing and Trailing Plants*, Collingridge 1957

Preston, George, *Climbing and wall plants*, 2nd edition, Cassell/The Royal Horticultural Society 1989

Rose, P.Q., *Ivies*, Blandford Press 1980

Rushforth, Keith, *Shrubs for small gardens*, Cassell/The Royal Horticultural Society, 1989

Thomas, G.S., *Climbing Roses Old and New*, Dent 1965

159

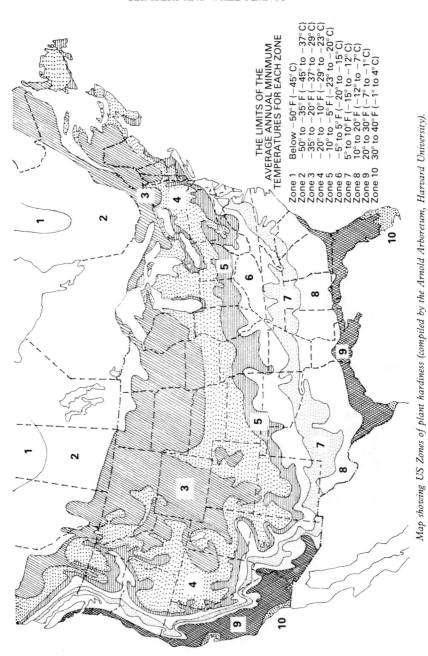

THE LIMITS OF THE
AVERAGE ANNUAL MINIMUM
TEMPERATURES FOR EACH ZONE

Zone 1   Below −50° F (−45° C)
Zone 2   −50° to −35° F (−45° to −37° C)
Zone 3   −35° to −20° F (−37° to −29° C)
Zone 4   −20° to −10° F (−29° to −23° C)
Zone 5   −10° to −5° F (−23° to −20° C)
Zone 6   −5° to 5° F (−20° to −15° C)
Zone 7   5° to 10° F (−15° to −12° C)
Zone 8   10° to 20° F (−12° to −7° C)
Zone 9   20° to 30° F (−7° to −1° C)
Zone 10  30° to 40° F (−1° to 4° C)

*Map showing US Zones of plant hardiness (compiled by the Arnold Arboretum, Harvard University).*

# Index of Scientific and Common Names

Figure in **bold** refer to colour plates.

161

# General Index

GENERAL INDEX